when

bad things

happen

when

bad things

happen

GOD IS BIG ENOUGH *to* HANDLE YOUR QUESTIONS...
and STRONG ENOUGH
TO DELIVER YOU *from* PAIN AND DOUBT

KAY ARTHUR

WATERBROOK
PRESS

WHEN BAD THINGS HAPPEN
PUBLISHED BY WATERBROOK PRESS
12265 Oracle Boulevard, Suite 200
Colorado Springs, Colorado 80921
A division of Random House, Inc.

Adapted from *Lord, Where Are You When Bad Things Happen?* Copyright © 1992, 2000.

All Scripture quotations, unless otherwise indicated, are taken from the
New American Standard Bible® (NASB), © Copyright The Lockman Foundation
1960, 1962, 1963, 1968, 1971, 1972, 1973, 1975, 1977, 1995. Used by permission.
(www.Lockman.org) Also quoted is the *King James Version*.

Italics in Scripture quotations reflect the author's added emphasis.

10 Digit ISBN: 1-60142-748-4
13 Digit ISBN: 978-1-60142-748-9

Copyright © 2002 by Kay Arthur

146655433

Contents

—◆—

Introduction

It's hard today to look at the chaos, at the tragedies, at the broken relationships, families, and lives—at the seeming triumph of evil men—and explain how God, if He is who He says He is, could allow these things. The question comes to mind, "Why doesn't He intervene, if He's God?"

If this is not your question, it certainly is the question of multitudes. Is there an answer? Is there an answer to the pain, the disappointment, the heartache, the death sentence you and countless others are facing? Yes, beloved, there is an answer—an answer you can stake your life on. You will find it in this book because it will take you to the Book of books, the Bible where God has the answers for every circumstance of life. This is why God has this book in your hands right now. He wants you to know and understand that He's there when bad things happen. Read on…

When you look at your circumstances and wonder,
"God, where are You?"

—∿—

He's There, Listening to the Cry of Your Heart

Open my eyes, that I may behold wonderful things from Your law.

PSALM 119:18

Has there ever been a time when you questioned God?

Possibly you found yourself in a trial you never dreamed would happen to you. Maybe you cried for help, and it seemed God didn't hear. You weren't delivered. You suffered.

When you watch the evening news or pick up the newspaper, do you wonder, *Where is God? If He is God and in charge of this universe, why does He allow the world to continue on its course of self-destruction? Why doesn't He put an end to all the cruel and bizarre things happening in our society?*

Did something happen to a child of God that seemed so unjust, so evil that you doubted God? Did you wonder, *Can't He at least take care of His own?* Maybe you wouldn't allow yourself

—∿—

to verbalize such a question because it would seem unholy, but have you wondered, *Where is God when bad things happen?*

A friend of mine was raped. She had heard me tell stories of others in similar situations who had called on God and were delivered. So in the darkness of fear she, too, cried out to God. In a trembling voice she commanded the man to stop in the name of Jesus. He didn't. Why didn't God answer her cry and deliver her?

Where was God?

A twenty-year-old girl, a personal friend of ours, a Christian with a sterling reputation, was found brutally murdered in her bedroom.

Where was God?

Hitler exterminated God's chosen people—men, women, and children—in gas chambers and ovens.

Where was God?

In countries with oppressive political systems, countless Christians suffer greatly for their faith. Denied the freedom to worship openly, many have been cut off from their communities and forced to live on almost nothing, enduring the ravages of malnutrition, beatings, and hard labor. Others have been imprisoned and tortured—even murdered by government edict—considered traitors simply because they placed their faith in Christ.

Where is God?

These are tough questions, aren't they? Skeptics delight in

asking these questions. They are questions many of us would prefer to ignore…or bury under weak and insufficient theological theories.

Where is God when bad things happen?

It's a question that many who call Him "Father" want to avoid. It doesn't fit with their concept of God. They can't explain it from the Word.

Are we afraid to ask these questions for fear God will not have an answer? Or do we fear that if we find the answer, it will distort our view of God or make Him into someone we cannot explain or understand?

Some would have you believe that God, who is a God of love, mercy, and compassion, does not have a thing to do with the evil that takes place in this world. But if He doesn't…then what does that imply about His power, His authority, His involvement in human affairs?

Are these new questions that, until now, have never troubled the heart of man? Oh no, my friend! They are as old as human history. They are the questions of Habakkuk, the prophet:

> How long, O LORD, will I call for help,
> And You will not hear?
> I cry out to You, "Violence!"
> Yet You do not save.
> Why do You make me see iniquity,

And cause me to look on wickedness?…
Why do You look with favor
On those who deal treacherously?
Why are You silent when the wicked swallow up
Those more righteous than they?
(Habakkuk 1:2-3,13)

Where is God? Why does He allow such things? Why does evil continue? Why do the wicked prosper? Why do the righteous suffer? Why aren't they delivered? Why doesn't God hear the prayers of His people? These questions are the burden of Habakkuk's heart. He bears them without shame or apology. And rather than ignoring them, God has preserved these questions for all to read. His answer to Habakkuk is also His answer to us.

Stop and read through the book of Habakkuk. It's only three chapters long. Before you begin reading, ask the Holy Spirit to guide you into the truth. We cannot understand and discern spiritual truths apart from His work in our lives. We need to ask the Lord to give us a spirit of wisdom and of revelation in the true knowledge of Him. We can be confident that He will answer because we have asked according to His will (1 John 5:14-15). Psalm 119:18 says, "Open my eyes, that I may behold wonderful things from Your law."

Pause a few moments to confess to the Lord your inability to hear and discern truth apart from His enabling. Ask Him to enlighten the eyes of your heart so that you may truly know what He longs to show you. Thank Him that He will.

GOD'S PEOPLE IN CRISIS

To appreciate the book of Habakkuk and how it parallels our day, we must consider its historical context. Not only will this perspective help you in grasping more of the meaning of the Old Testament, it will let you see how the truths of the Old Testament can be applied to our lives today! First Corinthians 10:11, in reference to Israel, says, "Now these things happened to them as an example, and they were written for *our* instruction, upon whom the ends of the ages have come."

After the death of Solomon, the nation of Israel was split into two kingdoms: the northern kingdom and the southern kingdom. The northern kingdom was composed of ten tribes and was called Israel. Israel turned to idolatry immediately after it split from the other two tribes. In 722 B.C., it fell to the Assyrians.

The southern kingdom was composed of the tribes of Judah and Benjamin. It is often referred to simply as Judah. Its capital was Jerusalem.

At the time Habakkuk was written, the northern kingdom had already gone into captivity.[1] Habakkuk prophesied sometime between 621 B.C. and 609 B.C. The Babylonian captivity of the southern kingdom was on the horizon in Habakkuk's time. It started in 605 B.C. when Nebuchadnezzar attacked Jerusalem and took a handful of nobles and princes to Babylon. Daniel was in that group.

Then in 597 B.C., when King Jehoiachin rebelled, Nebuchadnezzar again besieged Jerusalem and took ten thousand captive. Among that group was Ezekiel.

The final siege and destruction of Jerusalem occurred in 586 B.C., when the city and the temple were destroyed.

You may be wondering how the Israelites, God's beloved people, came to face such a crisis. After all, they were God's elect nation! Jerusalem was the home of Solomon's magnificent temple! Besides…who could be closer to the sovereign God of all the earth than Israel?

The answer, my friend, lies in their neglect of God's Word. The story of Judah reveals what happens when the Bible, the Word of God, loses center stage and is given a minor or "bit" part in the life of a nation or a church—or an individual.

Take a few minutes to read 2 Kings 22. Habakkuk, a contemporary of the prophet Jeremiah, probably would have witnessed the events related in this wonderful chapter, which opens around 622 B.C., a hundred years after the Assyrians had invaded and captured the northern kingdom. The current king of the southern kingdom was Josiah, who became king when he was eight years old.

Second Kings 22 focuses on the events that occurred in the

eighteenth year of Josiah's reign, when he was twenty-six years old. This makes the time about 622 B.C. Remember, Judah went into captivity in 586 B.C., thirty-six years later.

Shaphan the scribe was sent to clean and repair the damage in the temple of God. In the process of helping with these temple repairs, Hilkiah the high priest found a copy of God's Word. *Can you imagine?* The Word of God had been lost in the house of God!

Anguish struck Josiah's heart when Shaphan the scribe read aloud the Book of the Law. King Josiah saw how far the people of Judah had strayed from God's standard of holiness.

They had fallen into idolatry, worshiping Baal and Asherah (2 Kings 23:4). And wherever you find idolatry, you will find immorality or some sort of sexual perversion. One follows on the heels of the other. Second Kings 23:7 tells us that male cult prostitutes were living in the house of the Lord. They were part of the sexual immorality and perversion associated with Baal and Asherah worship.

This departure from the Word of God not only affected the morals of the people, it also endangered the lives of the children. In 2 Kings 23:10 we learn that parents made their children "pass through the fire for Molech." They offered blood sacrifices of their children on the altars of immorality.

Human sacrifice was not the only perversion. "God's people" had become involved in the occult and were also caught up in astrology (2 Kings 23:4-5), which was strictly forbidden by God in Deuteronomy 17:2-7. The people had turned to mediums, spiritists, and stars instead of consulting God. Behind idols, mediums, spiritists, and astrology, you will find demons (1 Corinthians 10:19-20).

How this must have hurt our Lord! Once Josiah heard God's Word, read by Shaphan the scribe, he understood the righteous wrath of God that had to be executed in holy judgment.

WHERE ARE WE HEADED?

You may well question how God's people could have strayed so far from His commands. But look around you. Is it any different today? No! But has it always been this way in the United States of America? No! In your lifetime you have seen great changes in what is condoned in America. Abortion used to be considered murder, and any doctor found performing an abortion was sentenced as a lawbreaker. Today, this form of child sacrifice has become a common means of birth control. Even many churches will not take a strong stand against abortion.

At one time homosexuality and lesbianism were against the law, but now the law promotes their "rights," including sanctioned marriage in certain states and adoption. Some in the church call homosexuality nothing more than a "genetic predisposition." Others have established homosexual congregations, saying God is against promiscuity but not homosexuality. They maintain that such behaviors merely reflect an alternative lifestyle.

At one time divorce wasn't tolerated in many denominations. Now, some in the church divorce, show up in church the next week with another spouse, and nothing is said. Church members are not held accountable for their behavior. For the most part, church discipline as set forth in 1 Corinthians 5 is no longer practiced.

Why are we in such a state? I believe it is because we've lost the Word of God—both in the house of God and in many seminaries. Many graduate from seminary with thorough training in the technicalities of ministry and of psychology, but they do not know how to study the Word and pray.

And consider this, beloved: If God's Word has been lost in many churches, how can we even expect the world to be aware of the righteous commandments in the Word?

So many write to tell me what has happened since they've started studying God's Word, learning it precept upon precept. As they've learned to dig out truth for themselves, their eyes have been opened to subtle errors that had crept into their thinking.

They see how they've been deluded by people's persuasive arguments, philosophies, and traditions.

They realize how they've bought into human reasoning and trendy teachings.

—∞—

They discern how, in recent years, psychology and self-preoccupation have replaced the Word and the Cross.

They find themselves able to quote and expound the latest Christian bestsellers, but not the Word of God.

They acknowledge that without the plumb line of God's Word, they could not perceive how far out of alignment they were from truth.

Thinking they were in touch with themselves, they realize they have been out of touch with God and His truth. They see how they have been deceived and how they have reaped the consequences of that deceit.

All of this happened because the Word of God had lost its proper place in their lives.

Think about it. What place, what priority, does the Word of God have in the lives of many pastors, let alone churchgoers? Has your church lost the Word of God? Have *you* lost it?

What happened in Judah can happen again. It's the inevitable result of losing the Word of God. Over and over again, church history testifies to the effects of neglecting the Word. The Church has been turned around only when a reformer has discovered, studied, lived by, and proclaimed the truths of God's Word in the hearing of His people.

Ask God to search your heart and show you if you have neglected the Word of God. Be honest and open before Him as you ask Him to show you what, if anything, has taken priority over

His Word. Ask Him what you need to do. Or, if you have given His Word its rightful place, spend time in worship and thanksgiving. Renew your commitment, so that in all things He will have the preeminence.

Believe me, dear one: Those who make it their lifestyle to study the Bible for themselves and apply its truths to their lives will never lose the Word of God again, for it will be at home in the temple of God (1 Corinthians 6:19). His Word will dwell in you richly (Colossians 3:16), and you'll not only be able to handle bad things that happen, but you'll be able to help others also.

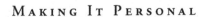

MAKING IT PERSONAL

So many times we question God or get angry or frustrated with Him for not meeting our expectations. In reality the heart of the problem is that we don't really know who God is. We don't understand God's ways because we haven't spent the time necessary to get to know Him and understand His perspective on life.

Do you think that's right? Would you want somebody to do that to you? Of course not! Wouldn't you want to say to that person, "Get to know me, listen to me, before you judge me. Then make your decision based on the facts"?

Oh, beloved, do you find yourself judging God when you really don't know Him that well? It is so easy to do when we are in pain or greatly disappointed. I think if you will spend time with God and get into His Word, you'll find yourself on your knees with tears of adoration and repentance streaming down your face. What pleasure this will bring to God—and you— when you know Him better.

When you realize you've been seeking satisfaction
in someone or something other than God…

—◦—

He's There—Tell Him You've Played the Fool and Run to His Open Arms

*Blessed is the man who trusts in the LORD and whose trust
is the LORD. For he will be like a tree planted by the water, that
extends its roots by a stream and will not fear when the
heat comes; but its leaves will be green, and it will not be
anxious in a year of drought nor cease to yield fruit.*

Jeremiah 17:7-8

When bad things happen, God gets our attention, doesn't He? In disasters such as the September 11, 2001, destruction of the twin towers of the World Trade Center, our thoughts turn immediately to the One who has power over all. Then we start to think about Him more and wonder if we should add Him into the equations of our lives, if we should change the way we live.

—◦—

REDISCOVERING GOD

The entire southern kingdom of Judah was scarred by sin—scarred because they had lost the Word of God. God was overlooked in the everyday issues of life in Israel in 622 B.C.; the people had all but forgotten Him. Then they found the book that had the answers, explained their sin and the judgment that was coming.

"Go, inquire of the LORD for me and the people and all Judah concerning the words of this book that has been found, for great is the wrath of the LORD that burns against us, because our fathers have not listened to the words of this book, to do according to all that is written concerning us," said King Josiah in 2 Kings 22:13.

What do you do when you suddenly see sin for what it is—when you suddenly become aware of a holy God who has every right to judge sin in His holy wrath?

Josiah's heart was tender to God's Word (2 Kings 22:19). He tore his clothes, humbled himself before God, and wept. No excuses, no covering up, no rationalizing, no blaming his sin or the sins of his people on another. Josiah owned Judah's sin. He took responsibility for it. Because of Josiah's heart, God heard his prayer and stayed His hand of judgment.

"Because your heart was tender and you humbled yourself before the LORD when you heard what I spoke against this place and against its inhabitants that they should become a desolation and a curse, and you have torn your clothes and wept before Me, I truly have heard you," declares the LORD. "Therefore, behold, I will gather you to your fathers, and you will be gathered to your grave in peace, and your eyes will not see all the evil which I will bring on this place." (2 Kings 22:19-20)

Hearing the Word of God brought a godly sorrow that led to repentance. "Before him there was no king like him who turned to the LORD with all his heart and with all his soul and with all his might, according to all the law of Moses; nor did any like him arise after him" (2 Kings 23:25).

What about you? When you sin, are you sorry? With what kind of sorrow? Oh, my friend, maybe your sin has been very great. But if you will do as Josiah did, if you will humble yourself before God and in godly sorrow turn from lawlessness to submission to God's Word, if you will turn to God with all your heart, soul, and might, God will meet you just as He met Josiah. The wrath of God will fall on the ungodly of this world, but it will not touch you. Whether wrath comes, as in Habakkuk's day, or whether people repent and revival comes, as it did in Josiah's day, you can rejoice in the God of your salvation…if you will but trust in God's Word.

PLAYING THE HARLOT

God honored Josiah's obedience. However, the hearts of the people did not change. "'Judah did not return to Me with all her heart, but rather in deception,' declares the LORD" (Jeremiah 3:10).

You would think the southern kingdom of Judah would have learned a lesson when the northern kingdom of Israel went into captivity under the Assyrians!

But Judah didn't heed that warning.

Why do we think we can deceive God and get away with it? Do we think God will exempt us from wholehearted obedience and fidelity to Him because we are His people? Do we think He would never allow the wicked to triumph over us because we profess Him and they don't?

Apparently that is what Judah thought, because when the false prophets proclaimed, "Peace, peace," the people loved what they said and believed their message (Jeremiah 5:30-31; 6:14). The temporary blessing and delayed judgment that came because of Josiah's repentance and obedience apparently lulled them into complacency, and they did not turn to God with all their hearts.

You may be hearing, "Peace, peace"...but is there peace deep within your heart? A peace that is not dependent upon your circumstances? If you want peace that the world cannot give and cannot take from you, make sure your relationship with God is what it ought to be. God must be your priority. Get rid of anything that hinders you from Him. When you refuse to give God first priority in your life, you deceive yourself.

What God spoke to Judah, He also speaks to you and me. As I've mentioned before, the things that were written before were written for our learning and admonition (see Romans 15:4). Listen to what God told Judah:

"Return, O faithless sons,
I will heal your faithlessness."…

"If you will return, O Israel," declares the LORD,
"Then you should return to Me.
And if you will put away your detested things
    from My presence,
And will not waver,
And you will swear, 'As the LORD lives,'
In truth, in justice, and in righteousness;
Then the nations will bless themselves in Him,
And in Him they will glory."

For thus says the LORD to the men of Judah and
    to Jerusalem,
"Break up your fallow ground,
And do not sow among thorns.
Circumcise yourselves to the LORD

And remove the foreskins of your heart,
Men of Judah and inhabitants of Jerusalem,
Or else My wrath will go forth like fire
And burn with none to quench it,
Because of the evil of your deeds."
(Jeremiah 3:22; 4:1-4)

According to God, His people had committed two evils. Listen to His words: "They have forsaken Me, the fountain of living waters," and they hewed "for themselves cisterns, broken cisterns that can hold no water" (Jeremiah 2:13).

God was to be their wellspring, the One to whom they turned for satisfaction, help, and guidance. They were to be dependent upon Him. A life lived in total dependence upon Him would be an expression of worship to Him that reflects the way in which He should be worshiped. Instead, they turned again to other sources.

In Jeremiah 2:18-19 God asked, "But now what are you doing on the road to Egypt, to drink the waters of the Nile? Or what are you doing on the road to Assyria, to drink the waters of the Euphrates? Your own wickedness will correct you, and your apostasies will reprove you; know therefore and see that it is evil and bitter for you to forsake the LORD your God, and the dread of Me is not in you."

I see Egypt as a picture of the world. The Israelites were the slaves of Egypt, under the dominion of Pharaoh. Similarly, until we come to know Jesus Christ personally, we are slaves of the world under the dominion of Satan, the prince of this world. Jesus is our Passover Lamb, the One whose blood was shed to deliver us from sin and death (see 1 Corinthians 5:7; Hebrews 2:14). Once the children of Israel were delivered by the Lord from the "land of Egypt, from the house of bondage" through the blood of the Passover Lamb, they were told to never return to Egypt. "Woe to those who go down to Egypt for help" (Jeremiah 34:13; Isaiah 31:1).

When God redeemed His people from Egypt, He told them exactly how they were to live. He set before them ten major commandments, along with many regulations for daily living.

The first commandment was to love Him above all else, "for I, the LORD your God, am a jealous God, visiting the iniquity of the fathers on the children, on the third and the fourth generations of those who hate Me, but showing lovingkindness to thousands, to those who love Me and keep My commandments" (Exodus 20:5-6).

God was their God. He would lead them, provide for them, protect them. They did not need to turn to the arm of flesh. Yet here they were in the days of Jeremiah and Habakkuk, running to drink the waters of the Nile and the Euphrates when they had access to the Fountain of Living Waters! This Old Testament example is parallel to you and me walking in the flesh instead of walking in the Spirit.

Water is necessary for life. Water has always been symbolic of God. Remember what happened during the Feast of Tabernacles? "Now on the last day, the great day of the feast, Jesus stood and cried out, saying, 'If anyone is thirsty, let him come to Me and drink. He who believes in Me, as the Scripture said, "From his innermost being will flow rivers of living water"'" (John 7:37-38).

In the Old Testament, God shows us that He alone is to be our life, our source, our sufficiency. Here in the New Testament, Jesus says the same thing. "Come" and "drink" are in the present tense in the Greek,[1] which implies continual or habitual action. You and I are to live in total dependence upon God.

But we don't always remember this, do we? We allow ourselves to be distracted, drawn away by the lust of our flesh, the lust of our eyes, and the pride of life. And our jealous God will not look lightly on such behavior. When we love something or someone else more than we love Him—whether it be a husband, wife, child, friend, profession, pleasure, or intellectual pursuit—God calls it harlotry.

To fail to love God above all else is to play the harlot with other lovers. This is why God said what He did to Jeremiah:

> Then the Lord said to me in the days of Josiah the king, "Have you seen what faithless Israel did? She went up on every high hill and under every green tree, and she was a harlot there. I thought, 'After she has done all these things,

she will return to Me'; but she did not return, and her treacherous sister Judah saw it. And I saw that for all the adulteries of faithless Israel, I had sent her away and given her a writ of divorce, yet her treacherous sister Judah did not fear; but she went and was a harlot also. Because of the lightness of her harlotry, she polluted the land and committed adultery with stones and trees. Yet in spite of all this her treacherous sister Judah did not return to Me with all her heart, but rather in deception," declares the LORD.

And the LORD said to me, "Faithless Israel has proved herself more righteous than treacherous Judah. Go, and proclaim these words toward the north and say,

> 'Return, faithless Israel,' declares the LORD;
> 'I will not look upon you in anger.
> For I am gracious,' declares the LORD;
> 'I will not be angry forever.
> Only acknowledge your iniquity,
> That you have transgressed against the LORD
>   your God
> And have scattered your favors to the strangers
>   under every green tree,
> And you have not obeyed My voice,' declares the
>   LORD.

—⁓—

'Return, O faithless sons,' declares the LORD;
'For I am a master to you,
And I will take you one from a city and two from
    a family,
And I will bring you to Zion.'" (Jeremiah 3:6-14)

Beloved, are you depending upon God, running to Him? If not, to whom are you turning? Are you turning to a person, to a position, to material possessions—what you drive, what you wear, where you live—to give you a sense of worth, value, purpose, acceptance, satisfaction? At what fountain are you drinking to quench your thirst? Has it really satisfied?

Have you played the harlot with God? Do you think, my friend, you can get away with it? You can't. Return to God with all of your heart, soul, mind, body, and strength.

MAKING IT PERSONAL

If you are feeling afflicted, if you suspect God is not pleased with you, maybe there are some things in your life that shouldn't be. Maybe you are feeling distressed or anxious, concerned about how God views your choices. If so, that's good, beloved. Feelings such as these stop us where we are and cause us to take a good look at ourselves, to evaluate where we are and where we are headed. Then we can make biblical adjustments to our lives.

In Psalm 119:67-68,71 we read:

> Before I was afflicted I went astray,
> But now I keep Your word.
> You are good and do good;
> Teach me Your statutes.
> It is good for me that I was afflicted,
> That I may learn Your statutes.

Why don't you take a minute and talk to God. Run into His arms like a child and say, "Abba, Father, You know where I am, what I'm dealing with, how I've played the fool. Restore me. Teach me Your Word, Your precepts of life, so I'll hate every false way."

When you find yourself asking,
"Who's in charge of this universe?"

—⦙⦙⦙—

He's There—
He Hasn't Left His
Sovereign Throne

The LORD of hosts has sworn saying,
"Surely, just as I have intended so it has happened,
and just as I have planned so it will stand.
For the LORD of hosts has planned, and who can frustrate it?
And as for His stretched-out hand, who can turn it back?"

ISAIAH 14:24,27

Have you ever been overwhelmed with grief—in such anguish, such despair, such confusion that you felt you couldn't go on? Have you ever been angry—just plain angry—because of a certain situation? Angry because you had no control over it? Or because of the injustice of it all? Or because what happened shouldn't have happened? Has anger welled up within…maybe even at God?

—⦙⦙⦙—

What do you do in situations like these? How do you handle your feelings? How do you survive and come out on top as a conqueror rather than being conquered?

Christians are not exempt from such feelings. Even the spiritually mature can encounter these experiences. And yet, my friend, you don't have to allow these situations to capture you and cast you into a prison of despair. You need to do what Habakkuk did.

When he was overwhelmed, Habakkuk embraced God. Although his situation never changed, as far as we know, he walked as a conqueror. With hinds' feet that did not slip, he walked above his circumstances on the high ground of faith (3:19).

The name *Habakkuk* means "one who embraces or caresses." When God seemed to ignore the sin of Judah, Habakkuk didn't bury the frustration he felt toward God. He expressed his anguish over God's seeming silence regarding the iniquity he beheld. He didn't conceal his feelings or questions under a cloak of spirituality. He didn't stuff them and deny that they burned in his heart. Rather, true to his name, Habakkuk brought it all out in the open and asked his God some hard questions. Then, in faith, he embraced what he knew about his covenant-keeping God and His Word.

Don't you know it touched the Father's heart to have His son Habakkuk embrace Him in faith's love? And say, in essence, "Father, I love you for Who You are, not just for what You can do for me or for what You will do for me. I love You no matter what…and, Father, I will trust you. I know You love me."

And you, beloved, need to do the same thing. Acknowledge where you are. (God knows anyway!) Then, in faith, embrace what you know about your God.

Do you feel as if God doesn't hear your prayers? Then cry out to Him and see how He answers in the days and weeks to come. God will speak! He may not change your circumstances or remove your burden, but through His Word He will bring you to the point where you can rejoice in Him and find Him as your strength.

You can rest in the knowledge that even when bad things happen, God is always there. He is always in charge. Although He may not always deliver in the way you expect, you will find His grace sufficient. Like the psalmist you can say:

> I sought the LORD, and He answered me,
> And delivered me from all my fears.
> They looked to Him and were radiant,
> And their faces will never be ashamed.
> This poor man cried, and the LORD heard him
> And saved him out of all his troubles.
> (Psalm 34:4-6)

Oh, my friend, will you embrace God in faith? Will you caress Him in unconditional love? Will you please Him with your faith? You were made in His image. God experiences emotion just as you do. Will you be a Habakkuk to your Father God? Tell Him so right now.

TRUSTING THE SOVEREIGNTY OF GOD

As we've seen, all of us face times of despair, periods of darkness when it seems as if we cannot find the strength to face yet another day of disappointment. When God doesn't seem to hear your cries or answer your prayers, you need to remember five principles.

We will explore each one so you might fully understand them and hide them in your heart. These truths will hold you in times of darkness, in times of trial and testing.

1. God is in control. He rules over the nations. He's in charge of history.

2. All history centers or pivots on two groups of people: Israel and the Church.

3. Whether or not we see it or understand it, there is a purpose in what God is doing.

4. Our times are in His hands.

5. Fear and doubt are conquered by a faith that rejoices.

Listen to Habakkuk in chapter 3:

> Though the fig tree should not blossom
> And there be no fruit on the vines,
> Though the yield of the olive should fail

And the fields produce no food,
Though the flock should be cut off from the fold
And there be no cattle in the stalls,
Yet I will exult in the LORD,
I will rejoice in the God of my salvation.
The Lord GOD is my strength,
And He has made my feet like hinds' feet,
And makes me walk on my high places.
(Habakkuk 3:17-19)

What confidence, trust, love, commitment! In all the Word of God, there is no greater declaration of faith. Habakkuk asked God hard questions. When God answered, Habakkuk submitted to Him in faith.

What enables a man or woman to make such a pledge of allegiance? It is the understanding of who God is and the realization that He is sovereign—that He accomplishes His plan, that nothing keeps Him from achieving His purpose.

My prayer for you and for me is that Habakkuk 3:17-19 will become our unwavering declaration of faith.

GOD IS IN CONTROL

Habakkuk asked God why He didn't hear his cry for help, why He let him see iniquity, violence, and destruction, and why He didn't deliver the righteous when He saw violence. Habakkuk couldn't understand why God allowed the wicked to surround the righteous and permitted justice to be perverted. Do his questions echo in your heart today?

Listen to God's response in Habakkuk 1:5: "Look among the nations! Observe! Be astonished! Wonder! Because I am doing something in your days—you would not believe if you were told."

Although Habakkuk hadn't seen it yet, God was doing something. He was raising up the Babylonians, a fierce, heathen nation that He would eventually use for His glorious, eternal purpose. He knew about and understood the iniquity, injustice, strife, and violence. And He was going to do something about it. Hard though it would be for Habakkuk to understand, God—who is in charge of history and, thus, rules over the nations—was going to use the Babylonians to judge His people Judah!

This thinking may present problems for you as you remember the many atrocities that men or nations have inflicted upon their fellow men—the insane cruelties of Hitler as he exterminated millions of Jews or the communist purges of the Chinese as they moved across that land. But please don't just close this book and walk away. Hear me out as I share with you what the Word of God teaches about God's sovereignty.

I believe that it was an understanding of the sovereignty of God that enabled Habakkuk to say what he did in Habakkuk 3:17-19. According to the *New American Standard Exhaustive*

Concordance of the Bible, in Habakkuk 3:19, he used the name "Lord GOD" to describe God. There the Hebrew word used for *Lord* is *Adonai,* which means "master, ruler." The Hebrew word for *God* is YHWH *(Yahweh),* which means "to be." Yahweh, or Jehovah, reveals God as the self-existent One. It is the most sacred of all the names of God. Therefore, when you combine these two names, *Adonai Yahweh,* the name can be translated as the *New International Version* translates it: Sovereign LORD.

Oh, beloved, when you can't understand what is going on and how God can allow such iniquity to exist without immediately intervening, you need to rest in the truth of God's sovereignty. No other truth has sustained me through all my trials and testings like the reality of God's sovereignty.

HISTORY IS IN HIS HANDS

Daniel 4:34-35 offers one of the clearest statements of God's sovereignty in all of Scripture. Let's examine it in the light of its context and see how it relates to Habakkuk and to the first principle we are considering for times of distress: *God is in control. He rules over the nations. He's in charge of history.*

God had told Habakkuk He was "raising up the Chaldeans [or Babylonians], that fierce and impetuous people" who would march throughout the earth to seize dwelling places and to eventually correct Judah for her sin (Habakkuk 1:6,12). The book of Daniel begins with an account of the beginning of the "day of distress." This was the day Habakkuk was to anticipate quietly as he waited "for the people to arise who will invade us" (Habakkuk 3:16).

The book of Daniel begins, "In the third year of the reign of Jehoiakim king of Judah, Nebuchadnezzar king of Babylon came to Jerusalem and besieged it. The Lord *gave* Jehoiakim king of Judah into his hand" (Daniel 1:1-2). God *gave* Jehoiakim over to the Babylonians just as He told Habakkuk He would.

As we discussed earlier, there were three sieges of Jerusalem before it was finally destroyed in 586 B.C. You'll remember that Daniel was taken captive in the first siege. Shortly afterward King Nebuchadnezzar came to realize and recognize the sovereignty of God. Daniel 4, either dictated or handwritten by the king, tells how he came to acknowledge God's sovereignty.

Nebuchadnezzar was given a dream from God "in order that the living may know that the Most High is ruler over the realm of mankind, and bestows it on whom He wishes, and sets over it the lowliest of men" (Daniel 4:17).

God spoke very clearly about His sovereignty to Nebuchadnezzar, not only through this dream but also through a clear and frightening interpretation. Yet it didn't sink in: "Twelve months later he was walking on the roof of the royal palace of Babylon. The king reflected and said, 'Is this not Babylon the great, which I myself have built as a royal residence by the might of my power and for the glory of my majesty?'" (Daniel 4:29-30).

Nebuchadnezzar isn't very different from other men, is he? We think we are the captains of our fate. We think we determine our own destiny. We forget that "every good thing given and every perfect gift is from above, coming down from the Father of lights" (James 1:17), and that God "does according to His will in the host of heaven and among the inhabitants of earth" (Daniel 4:35).

But the Lord will not allow us to continue in such folly. Nebuchadnezzar's arrogance resulted in God taking away all that he had boasted about. The king lost his reason and became as a beast of the field, a wild animal. For seven years he ate grass and lived in the field with the cattle. Imagine the terror and humiliation!

After God humbled Nebuchadnezzar by letting him lose his mind, He brought the king back to his senses. As a result, Nebuchadnezzar wrote these words about God: "For His dominion is an everlasting dominion, and His kingdom endures from generation to generation. And all the inhabitants of the earth are accounted as nothing, but He does according to His will in the host of heaven and among the inhabitants of earth; and no one can ward off His hand or say to Him, 'What have You done?'" (Daniel 4:34-35).

Oh, beloved, God is telling us He rules over all that is in heaven and on earth. This rule includes not only the cherubim, the seraphim, and the good angels, but encompasses every demon and the prince of the power of the air, Satan himself! Neither

Satan nor his demons can ever do anything to you apart from God's permission!

Therefore, according to 1 Corinthians 10:13, whatever comes into your life will never be more than you can bear! Wow! No wonder you can be more than a conqueror through Jesus Christ in every circumstance of life (Romans 8:35-39)!

Not only is it true that you can live as a conqueror, but since God does according to His will among the inhabitants of the earth, no one on earth can do anything to you without God's permission. This truth means that no human being can overpower or surprise God. This truth also reveals the reason you can rejoice in God no matter what. "In everything give thanks; for this is God's will for you in Christ Jesus" (1 Thessalonians 5:18).

Because God is sovereign, He can promise that *all* things will work together for good for those who love Him, for those who are called according to *His purpose.* For those whom He foreknows, He predestines to become conformed to the image of His Son (Romans 8:28-29). Because God is sovereign, even when people intend to do evil against you, God will work it out for your good. He is the Redeemer of the difficulties, trials, and tragedies of life.

FILTERED THROUGH FINGERS OF LOVE

I wasn't saved until I was twenty-nine years old. By then I was a mess—a poor picture of what God intended a woman to be.

I wanted to be perfect, but I wasn't.

I tried to be good, but I couldn't.

I thought I was a Christian, but I wasn't.

I was merely religious.

The one thing I wanted in life—to be happily married—had eluded me. The perfect marriage, the perfect family, the perfect home were dreams that never became reality.

At twenty-nine I was a divorcée with two precious sons. It was a divorce of my own doing. But it was the undoing of me. Without the restraints of marriage and consumed by a passion to be loved, I became an immoral woman.

Finally, I saw myself as I really was: a slave to sin. On July 16, 1963, I came to know the Lord Jesus Christ and became a new creature. How awed I was by the changes the Holy Spirit made in my life! Next to being able to say no to sin, the greatest excitement was in reading God's Word and being able to understand it. I did not know at the time that this is the birthright of every child of God (1 Corinthians 2:9-16).

After I came to know Jesus Christ, God sent a godly man to tutor me in the faith. I was like a dry sponge being softened by the Word, absorbing all I could get. One night as Dave and I sat in my living room, he took off his signet ring and put it into his hand, clinching his fingers around it until his knuckles were white. Then he said, "Kay, now that you belong to Jesus Christ, you are just like this ring and my hand is just like the hand of

God. God has you in His hand. No one can touch you, look at you, or speak to you without God's permission."

I didn't recognize it then, but Dave was teaching me about the sovereignty of God. Later, as I came to understand that God is sovereign—in control of all so that nothing can happen without His knowledge or permission—I understood more fully what Dave had been saying.

I also came to understand that the God who held me in His sovereign hand is a God of love (1 John 4:10). Everything that came into my life would have to be filtered through His fingers of love.

"Filtered through fingers of love" became a phrase I would pass down to my students so that they, too, could cling to it through their trials.

When I wanted to marry Dave, and counselors told him not to marry me because I was divorced, I clung to this truth.

When I told God I'd go back and marry my ex-husband and then faced his suicide before I could tell him of my willingness to come home, I clung to this truth.

God is in control. He rules over all. He loves me. He desires my highest good.

Oh, dear child of God, do you see that no matter what happens in your life, in your family, or in your nation, you, like Habakkuk, can rejoice in the God of your salvation? Everything in your life is filtered through His fingers of love.

Isn't understanding God's sovereignty exciting, awesome, comforting? Are you understanding more clearly why Habakkuk could say what he did in 3:17-19? No matter what happens, because God is sovereign, you can live above it all with hinds' feet on high places—if you are His child.

Once you understand and embrace what the Bible teaches about the character and sovereignty of God, you will find calm in the center of life's storms.

Your understanding of the fact that God rules over all—that there are no accidents in life, that no tactic of Satan or man can ever thwart the will of God—should bring divine comfort.

Then it is easy to understand how the promise of Romans 8:28-30 can be true: "And we know that God causes all things to work together for good to those who love God, to those who are called according to His purpose. For those whom He foreknew, He also predestined to become conformed to the image of His Son, so that He would be the firstborn among many brethren; and these whom He predestined, He also called; and these whom He called, He also justified; and these whom He justified, He also glorified."

When you grasp and bow to the truth of how all things are working together for good to conform you to His image, then in faith you are able to rejoice and give thanks in all things, knowing that this is the will of God in Christ Jesus concerning you (1 Thessalonians 5:18).

Stop right now and thank Him in faith.

MAKING IT PERSONAL

Every time something bad happens, teach yourself to say to God, "Almighty God, Psalm 103:19 says Your sovereignty rules over all—even my mistakes—and that eventually You will use this to make me more like Jesus. Therefore I will trust You right now. Show me where to go from here."

If you will do this, beloved, it will bring a peace that passes all understanding and the confidence to go on.

When the world appears to be
crumbling around you...

—⚬—

He's There—Remember
Who He Is

He only is my rock and my salvation, my stronghold;
I shall not be shaken. On God my salvation and my glory rest;
the rock of my strength, my refuge is in God.

PSALM 62:6-7

Life may seem so frustrating, overwhelming, and futile to you
right now that you're tempted to check out.

Maybe you have thought of walking away, running away,
leaving it all—maybe having an affair or getting a divorce. Have
you been tempted to forget holiness and pursue happiness or to
compromise your convictions because it doesn't seem to do you
any good to live righteously? Maybe you feel your convictions
have just left you poor or lonely. Maybe you are thinking of sell-
ing out to the pressure and saying yes. Or maybe you're thinking
of just ending it all, escaping in death's sweet peace. But will it be
peace—or hell?

—⚬—

Maybe…maybe…maybe.

Do you ever think maybes like these? It's not healthy, my friend. The Bible calls these "imaginations" or "speculations" (2 Corinthians 10:5). If they get ahold of you, they can devastate or destroy you.

Second Corinthians 10:3-6 teaches that we are in a war and that the warfare is for our minds. As a man thinks in his heart, so he is (Proverbs 23:7). The enemy of your soul, the devil, knows this. That's why he targets your mind with his poison arrows. Satan wants you to think contrary to the character of God and the Word of God. His tactics are to accuse God and others. He wants to persuade you to act independently of God, to walk according to the flesh rather than the Spirit.

Maybes that aren't in accord with God's Word are lies. They are Satan's alternatives to total obedience to God. They are short-cuts to happiness that, if pursued by man, bring only misery—a living hell.

The cure for such maybes is to focus on the certainties of the character of your God and, in faith, embrace all that He is. Bring every thought captive to the obedience of Jesus Christ by casting down imaginations and every high thought that is raised up against the knowledge of God (2 Corinthians 10:5).

Habakkuk did what you and I must do when things are too hard for us to reconcile, to understand, and, therefore, to accept. He rehearsed the attributes of God. Because he remembered who his God was, he was able to walk in faith—even though he couldn't fully understand how and why God was doing what He was doing. Watch carefully what Habakkuk did. There will come a time, beloved, when you will need to do likewise. It may even be now.

In Habakkuk 1:12-13, the prophet said,

> "Are You not from everlasting,
> O LORD, my God, my Holy One?
> We will not die.
> You, O LORD, have appointed them to judge;
> And You, O Rock, have established them to
>   correct.
> Your eyes are too pure to approve evil,
> And You can not look on wickedness with favor."

What did Habakkuk call to mind about God?

THE IMMOVABLE, ETERNAL ROCK

First, he remembered that God is eternal. God is from everlasting to everlasting—the beginning and the end (Revelation 21:6). He always has been and He always will be. If He is eternal, then all things find their beginning and end in Him. "All things came into being through Him, and apart from Him nothing came into being that has come into being" (John 1:3). "For from Him and through Him and to Him are all things" (Romans 11:36).

One thing will always remain: God. And because He is immutable (unchanging), He will always be the same. Your spouse, children, parents, and loved ones may be taken away, but God will always be there. He will never leave you nor forsake you (Hebrews 13:5).

Habakkuk addresses God, "And You, O Rock, have established them to correct" (1:12). From the time Moses struck the rock in the wilderness, causing water to flow freely, God had been known as the Rock. Paul tells us in 1 Corinthians that when the children of Israel came out of Egypt they "all drank the same spiritual drink, for they were drinking from a spiritual rock which followed them; and the rock was Christ" (1 Corinthians 10:4).

Because we find ourselves living in the midst of a violent, destructive, sinful, unstable society, it is critical that we carefully build our lives on the Rock of who He is and then learn to run to the Rock who is higher than we are. If we will live in this manner, we will find ourselves able to live stable, consistent lives, unmoved by all the problems around us.

Oh, friend, don't you see? No matter what the changes in your life, in your family, in your nation, there is always one stabilizing factor upon which you can rest: your God. He is the immovable Rock. You can hide in Him.

He is always there with arms opened wide, your everlasting Father God.

The eternity of God was the first attribute that Habakkuk called to mind. Precious child of God, why don't you simply meditate on the fact that, although your history may change, God will not? He is everlasting. He can bring stability to your life. Claim that in faith.

THE GREAT I AM

Not only is God everlasting, He is also self-existent. As we've learned, YHWH (Yahweh) is the Hebrew name of God that reveals Him as the great I AM, the self-existent One. YHWH is usually rendered LORD all in capital letters in the *New American Standard Bible.*

Take a few minutes and read Exodus 3. Be sure to note how Moses responded when God appeared to him at the burning bush and told him He was sending him to deliver the Israelites from the land of Egypt, from the house of bondage.

If "I AM" is God's memorial name to *all* generations, that includes *your* generation as well! He is *your* great I AM—"I AM everything and anything you will ever need." Isn't that exciting? If we would only believe it and live accordingly.

"The name of the LORD is a strong tower; the righteous runs

into it and is safe," says Proverbs 18:10. We see Habakkuk do exactly that when he reminds himself of who God is. Focusing on who God is enabled Habakkuk to live as more than a conqueror in very dark days. How clear this is in Habakkuk 3:18, when the prophet declared in faith, "Yet I will exult in the LORD, I will rejoice in the God of my salvation." Once again he used the name YHWH, the great I AM.

Habakkuk's existence and welfare did not depend on fig trees, fruit, olives, fields yielding crops, or on cattle in the stalls. His existence depended on his YHWH, the self-existent I AM. I AM would always be there as Habakkuk's strength, giving him hinds' feet that would not slip. His I AM would enable him to live above his circumstances, whatever they might be.

Because God does not change, He will do the same for you. He is to you as He was to Habakkuk—everything that you will ever need, your I AM. You will discover this reality moment by moment as you exult in who He is!

THE CREATOR

Habakkuk also remembered that the Lord was his Elohim. Habakkuk said, "Are You not from everlasting, O LORD, my God, my Holy One?" (Habakkuk 1:12). This Hebrew word for *God* used in Habakkuk 1:12 is the name used for God in His role as Creator.

As you focus on God as Elohim, you are reminded in Hebrews 11:3 that "the worlds were prepared by the word of God, so that what is seen was not made out of things which are visible." God is the One who is in control, the One whose Word is so powerful that it brought a universe into existence. If God can create the universe with a word, can't He also subdue all things by the Word of His power when He is ready to do so? Of course!

As Elohim, He created all things. "All things have been created through Him and for Him" (Colossians 1:16). Because of this truth, my friend, maybes are not our rightful option. Rather, we are called to submission. No matter what happens, we need to say, "Father, I exist because of You and for You. Therefore, not my will but Yours be done."

THE RIGHTEOUS JUDGE

Not only is God the everlasting self-existent Creator, He is also the Holy One of Israel. Habakkuk brought this fact to God's remembrance when God informed him that He would judge Judah. When Satan's fiery darts are aimed at your mind, rehearse God's holiness. So often when things go wrong, man wants to blame God. But can a holy God do what is wrong?

Holiness is total purity without any taint of evil or wrong-doing. And what makes God holy? It is the sum total of all His attributes, making Him totally other than man. Because God is holy, He can do no wrong. If He did, He would not be holy. Therefore, whatever Habakkuk's conception of what God was doing in allowing such evil to abound, he knew it could not contradict the truth about God. And Habakkuk knew that God was holy! Habakkuk could not judge God as being unjust in what His sovereignty permitted.

And neither can you, my friend. If you'll remember that, you'll walk in faith and save yourself a lot of grief.

In reminding God of who He was, Habakkuk saw that because of God's holiness He was allowing the Babylonians to correct Judah. "Are You not from everlasting, O LORD, my God, my Holy One? We will not die. You, O LORD, have appointed them to judge; and You, O Rock, have established them to correct" (Habakkuk 1:12).

THE GOD OF THE COVENANT

Why did Habakkuk know that they would not die even though God would judge them in righteousness? What did Habakkuk mean by the term "die"? Surely when the Babylonians went up against God's chosen in battle, people would die!

Yes, some would die physically. But Israel would not die as a nation; the nation would not be wiped out. I believe this is what Habakkuk meant. Habakkuk knew that God was immutable, that He would not change. Habakkuk knew that His God was a *beriyth* covenant-keeping God.

The English translation of the Hebrew word *beriyth* is *covenant*. The word means "a compact or agreement made by passing through pieces of flesh." If two people entered into a covenant, they entered into a solemn, binding agreement.

In Genesis 15:9-21 when God alone—and not Abraham— passed through the pieces in the image of a flaming torch and a smoking oven, He was signifying that this was a covenant that would not be broken. On that day God swore by Himself that the land would be Israel's forever. This covenant was later confirmed to Isaac and Jacob.

In Exodus 2:24 when the sons of Israel sighed and cried out to God because of their bondage in Egypt, "God heard their groaning; and God remembered His covenant with Abraham, Isaac, and Jacob," and He sent Moses to deliver them.

Because God is a covenant-keeping God, because He can neither lie nor alter the words that have gone forth from His mouth, Israel will always remain a nation. Because Habakkuk grasped this truth by faith, he knew they would not die. God would chasten them as a nation, but He would not exterminate them as a people.

Even before the final Babylonian siege of Jerusalem, God sent word through a letter from Jeremiah to those in exile, giving them this promise: " 'When seventy years have been completed for Babylon, I will visit you and fulfill My good word to you, to bring you back to this place. For I know the plans that I have for you,' declares the LORD, 'plans for welfare and not for calamity to give you a future and a hope' " (Jeremiah 29:10-11). God would keep His covenant.

CHILD OF GOD, CHILD OF COVENANT

A friend of mine once suffered a total breakdown. Because of a certain sin she had committed, she felt God could not forgive her. What a lie from the enemy! When you sin as a child of God, God will discipline you, but He will never forsake you nor abandon you (Hebrews 13:4-5). God never casts off His own. How vital it is that you remember this truth.

We know that Habakkuk understood and rested in this truth because he said, "We will not die" (Habakkuk 1:12). Habakkuk knew God was a covenant-keeping God.

If you are a believer, a true child of God, a new creature in Christ Jesus, you are in covenant with Jesus Christ. Do you remember what Jesus did on the night that He was betrayed?

> While they were eating, Jesus took some bread, and after a blessing, He broke it and gave it to the disciples, and said, "Take, eat; this is My body." And when He had taken a

cup and given thanks, He gave it to them, saying, "Drink from it, all of you; for this is My blood of the covenant, which is poured out for many for forgiveness of sins. But I say to you, I will not drink of this fruit of the vine from now on until that day when I drink it new with you in My Father's kingdom." (Matthew 26:26-29)

Did you note that Jesus assured His disciples they would drink the cup with Him once again "in My Father's kingdom"? What was Jesus promising them? He was saying, in essence, that the covenant into which they were entering would guarantee that one day they would spend eternity together in the Father's kingdom.

Did this promise mean they would never sin again? No! It meant that because they believed in Him, sin's power to rule their lives would be broken and they would have forgiveness of sins and eternal life. That was the covenant of grace. Not grace that would give them license to live in sin, but grace that would enable them by the gift of the Holy Spirit to overcome the law of sin and death. When they did sin, they were to confess their sins and God would be "faithful and just to forgive" their sins and to cleanse them from all unrighteousness (1 John 1:9, KJV).

When God disciplines you, that doesn't mean He has forsaken you; remember, He has made a covenant with you. Like Habakkuk, you must know you "will not die"; God will not cast you off forever. God is simply acting according to His character and fulfilling His purpose. "When we are judged, we are disciplined by the Lord so that we will not be condemned along with the world" (1 Corinthians 11:32).

Going back to my friend who had the breakdown, how I would love to put my arms around her and tell her that God could never fail to forgive her. For Him not to forgive would be to go against His covenant! He loves her with an everlasting love, and, like Israel, the plans He has for her are plans for her welfare and her good, to give her a future and a hope.

Beloved, we need to remember that God is the Rock! When the storms of affliction come and the winds of violence blow against us, like David, we can run to the Rock that is higher than you and I and declare with certainty:

> The LORD is my rock and my fortress and my
>   deliverer;
> My God, my rock, in whom I take refuge....
>
> The LORD lives, and blessed be my rock;
> And exalted be God, the rock of my salvation,
> The God who executes vengeance for me,
> And brings down peoples under me,
> Who also brings me out from my enemies;
> You even lift me above those who rise up
>   against me;

You rescue me from the violent man.
Therefore I will give thanks to You, O LORD,
    among the nations,
And I will sing praises to Your name.
He is a tower of deliverance to His king,
And shows lovingkindness to His anointed,
To David and his descendants forever.
(2 Samuel 22:2-3,47-51)

How I pray that you will be able to say with David, "He only is my rock and my salvation, my stronghold; I shall not be shaken. On God my salvation and my glory rest; the rock of my strength, my refuge is in God" (Psalm 62:6-7).

MAKING IT PERSONAL

So many times when tragedy comes, we think we can't live through it, but we can—even if it involves a "death sentence," news that we don't have long to live. Remember, child of God, your Father has made a covenant with you; you will spend eternity with Him—no matter what happens here on earth.

If you will memorize 1 Corinthians 10:13, the Spirit of God will use it to remind you that whatever the temptation, the trial, the tragedy, or the test, you can bear it. Then you will run to God, seeking His way of escape.

No temptation has overtaken you but such as is common to man; and God is faithful, who will not allow you to be tempted beyond what you are able, but with the temptation will provide the way of escape also, so that you will be able to endure it. (1 Corinthians 10:13)

When your hopes are frustrated
and life disappoints…

—⟋⟍—

He's There—There's a Purpose in It All

"For My thoughts are not your thoughts, neither are your ways
My ways," declares the LORD. "For as the heavens are higher
than the earth, so are My ways higher than your ways,
and My thoughts than your thoughts."

Isaiah 55:8-9

How can you have a triumphant faith when life is so full of stress?
How do you watch all that is taking place around you without
falling apart?

It's all a matter of perspective.

Our second principle gives that perspective: *History centers on*
two groups of people—the nation of Israel and the Church of Jesus
Christ. God is in charge of history; it is His story. And all that He
does pivots on Israel or the Church.

When stressful times smash into our lives, we need to ask,
"What is God doing in my life, in the Church, or in the nation

—⟋⟍—

of Israel?" All that happens will somehow relate to God's purpose for Israel or for His Church.

I remember when a drought hit the United States a number of summers ago. Driving through Atlanta, I saw a sign in front of a business that read "Pray for Rain." I was impressed that someone realized where rain came from. Yet as I thought about it, I felt we needed to go a step beyond praying for rain and ask God why He had withheld the rain.

Could it be because of our sin? Was God trying to speak to America, to His Church? To draw us to our knees in repentance? To remind us that it is "the LORD our God, who gives rain in its season, both the autumn rain and the spring rain, who keeps for us the appointed weeks of the harvest" (Jeremiah 5:24)?

All of history—including the famines, droughts, plagues, and economic disasters—centers on what God wants to bring to pass regarding either Israel or the Church. Sometimes we forget that God is moving throughout the nations of the earth, calling out a people for Himself.

He uses all sorts of means to bring people to their knees, so they might see that He is the Lord God and that they need to worship Him and submit to the lordship of His Son. Whatever means He uses is worth the pain, if it causes us to pass from death to life by believing on His Son. "Or do you think lightly of the riches of His kindness and tolerance and patience, not knowing that the kindness of God leads you to repentance?" (Romans 2:4).

Your whole perspective on current events can change if you know that the God who is in charge of history is working everything according to His purpose for Israel and for the Church—not only for those who have already heard His voice but also for those who have yet to believe.

We see this truth in the book of Habakkuk. A whole nation had been raised up by God and given a place of world dominance simply to act as a rod of discipline. God "established them [the Babylonians] to correct" (Habakkuk 1:12).

Before the Babylonians were ever a world power, God said to Israel, "If you diligently obey the LORD your God…the LORD your God will set you high above all the nations of the earth" (Deuteronomy 28:1).

With that promise, God spoke through Moses to tell them the blessings that would be theirs, including the promise that He would cause all their enemies to be defeated before them!

Along with that promise of blessing, however, came the assurance of cursing for disobedience: "But it shall come about, if you do not obey the LORD your God, to observe to do all His commandments and His statutes with which I charge you today, that all these curses will come upon you and overtake you" (Deuteronomy 28:15).

Among the curses identified in Deuteronomy 28, we find this:

> The LORD will bring a nation against you from afar…a nation of fierce countenance who will have no respect for the old, nor show favor to the young. Moreover, it shall eat the offspring of your herd and the produce of your ground until you are destroyed, who also leaves you no grain, new wine, or oil, nor the increase of your herd or the young of your flock. (Deuteronomy 28:49-51)

God also told them that the enemy would lay siege against them, moving the Israelites to eat their own children (Deuteronomy 28:53-57).

Awful, isn't it? Yet, because they refused to obey, that is exactly what happened. And how did Habakkuk handle the stress of it all? He saw the bigger picture. He knew that God would have to judge Israel, but he also knew that, by faith, he could live above the stress.

Beloved, you can do the same. Instead of being frustrated and overwhelmed by all that is going on in our world, go to the Lord and ask Him to give you His eternal perspective. Like Habakkuk, keep watch in the Word of God and allow Him to speak to you (Habakkuk 2:1). Live by what you know from God's Word rather than by your present experiences.

God's Perspective Is Broader

Have you ever wrestled with why the wicked seem to prosper and why the righteous seem not to prosper?

Even after Habakkuk confirmed in his heart that God was from everlasting, his Creator, his Holy One, and his Rock, he was still troubled. How could his God allow such wicked and treacherous men like the Babylonians to be His instrument for judging the covenant nation? It was perplexing and disturbing. Was God going to allow the Babylonians to "empty their net [of their catch of men] and continually slay nations without sparing" (Habakkuk 1:17)?

At this point Habakkuk had to get alone with God and wait for His answer. Can you relate to that? Are there times when life just doesn't seem right, fair, equitable? You ask yourself, *Does it really pay to be a Christian, to live a holy life?*

What you are going through is not unique. Habakkuk wrestled with it. So did Asaph, whose wrestlings are recorded for us in Psalm 73. In that passage of Scripture he shared how his feet came close to stumbling because he was envious of the arrogant as he saw their prosperity. They denied that God even knew what was going on. They were at ease, increasing in wealth, while Asaph suffered continually.

Asaph could not reason all of this out. Finally he did as Habakkuk did. He went to God for His perspective. He had to get alone, go into the sanctuary of God, and let God speak to him. Then Asaph, like Habakkuk, got a proper perspective on life.

Both saw the end of unrighteous men, the judgment of God upon the wicked. Then they understood that God was all they needed. Habakkuk saw God as his strength, his enabler. Asaph wrote: "Whom have I in heaven but You? And besides You, I desire nothing on earth. My flesh and my heart may fail, but God is the strength of my heart and my portion forever.... The nearness of God is my good" (Psalm 73:25-26,28).

Beloved, I want you to have time alone with God. In nearness to Him, you can get His perspective on life so that you know how to live. I pray you will take time to meditate on what you have learned so that its truth becomes bone of your bones and flesh of your flesh.

It's All in Accordance with God's Plan

The third principle we need to consider is this: *There is a purpose in what God does.* Whether we understand or not, our God is working, and He knows what He is doing! What He is doing will always work together for the good of the individual Christian, the Church, and the nation of Israel.

When Habakkuk unloaded his burden on God, asking why He hadn't heard his cry for help and why He allowed all the wickedness that he saw, God assured Habakkuk that He was working. Read Habakkuk 1:5 again: "Look among the nations! Observe! Be astonished! Wonder! Because I am doing something in your days—you would not believe if you were told."

Habakkuk didn't know or understand it. And as a matter of fact, Habakkuk would have had a hard time even believing it. But God was working! God was carrying out His plan and His purpose in history.

Isaiah 14:24 and 27 are such comforting and pertinent verses that I want to encourage you to meditate on them: "The LORD of hosts has sworn saying, 'Surely, just as I have intended so it has happened, and just as I have planned so it will stand.... For the LORD of hosts has planned, and who can frustrate it? And as for His stretched-out hand, who can turn it back?' "

Oh, beloved, do you see it? From the destiny of the nations to the destiny of your life, God is in control. He has a plan, and that plan is according to His purpose in your life. His purpose is to make you into the image of His Son, the Lord Jesus Christ. Nothing can frustrate or abort God's plans, either for Israel, the Church, the nations, or you.

Stop and think about it. Like Habakkuk, you may not think God is working, but He is. Believe Him, and you will have an overcoming faith.

Read and meditate on Romans 8:37-39:

But in all these things we overwhelmingly conquer through Him who loved us. For I am convinced that neither death, nor life, nor angels, nor principalities, nor things present, nor things to come, nor powers, nor height, nor depth, nor any other created thing, will be able to separate us from the love of God, which is in Christ Jesus our Lord.

It's All in Accordance with God's Character

Sometimes we shipwreck our faith by thinking that God is like man. We begin to evaluate His actions on the basis of how we would behave if we were God. We judge God from man's perspective.

For instance, when we hear of disasters in which thousands are killed and we say, "But a loving God wouldn't do that," we evaluate His actions according to our concept of love.

We tend to evaluate everything from the realm of our experiences with other human beings. We measure God by how others think, respond, react, perform, or love. Then, if we don't know the Word of God or if we do not stop to consider and believe what it says, we think that God is going to act—or *ought* to act— in the same way as man.

Also, we often fail to look at the sum total of God's attributes. We isolate some of them, forgetting that what God does is always and totally consistent with who He is.

We forget God's ways are not our ways, nor His thoughts our thoughts.

> "For My thoughts are not your thoughts,
> Nor are your ways My ways," declares the LORD.
> "For as the heavens are higher than the earth,
> So are My ways higher than your ways,
> And My thoughts than your thoughts."
> (Isaiah 55:8-9)

In other words, He is God. Transcendent. Holy. Incomprehensible. We cannot sit in judgment or evaluate God and His actions because we are finite. We are limited in our thinking, in our knowledge, in our experience, in our ability, and in the brevity of our lives.

Remember, God is at work and He will always act according to His character, not man's. He can never divorce Himself from who He is, nor can He act contrary to His character. "If we are faithless, He remains faithful, for He cannot deny Himself" (2 Timothy 2:13).

Because of this glorious truth, dear child of God, you can

know with absolute certainty that while nothing else may be consistent in your life, God is. He is immutable; He does not change.

FAITH WAITS WITH LISTENING EARS

Many Christians have waged war on their knees against evil rulers and nations, only to see the malicious conquests continue. Where was God? Why wasn't He hearing their prayers?

Would these Hitlers of history continue unchecked forever as they sought to annihilate the chosen of God, Jews and Christians?

How can a righteous and holy God allow "the wicked [to] swallow up those more righteous than they?" (Habakkuk 1:13). Habakkuk could understand how God had to judge Judah, but why would He allow these evil men to treat those whom they conquered with as little value as fish in the sea, dragging them away with their net, slaying them without sparing? Would God never stop them, never bring their wickedness to a halt (Habakkuk 1:14-17)?

Have you ever felt the same way? Have you ever felt as if your prayers were useless because the actions of wicked men continued unchecked? Did you want to give up? Quit praying? Walk away and forget it all? When you find yourself unable to understand the ways of God, or when you find yourself frustrated because God does not seem to be hearing, you must learn a lesson from Habakkuk. Listen to what he did:

—

I will stand on my guard post
And station myself on the rampart;
And I will keep watch to see what He will speak
    to me,
And how I may reply when I am reproved.
(Habakkuk 2:1)

Habakkuk didn't quit. Habakkuk *waited*…with a listening ear. Despair walks away, thinking God doesn't care. Faith waits and listens, knowing that in God's perfect time He will speak. Silence does not mean that God has abandoned you or that He does not care. It doesn't mean that God is like man, showing anger by refusing to communicate. When God is silent, it simply means that He has, for some reason, not yet chosen to say any more. Yet in the silence He is still fulfilling His purpose. He is still acting according to His character and sovereignty—whether we understand or not.

Waiting is hard. Silence is even harder. And yet we can endure in faith, beloved, if you and I will only remember that, although the wicked seemingly go unchecked, God is in control. He is in charge of history. Therefore, whatever is happening will somehow work out for the good of Israel or the Church.

There is a purpose in what God is doing. When He is ready to tell us, He will. Until then, like Habakkuk, we need to keep the watch of faith, to see what God will say to us.

MAKING IT PERSONAL

God never leaves His children in the dark. He does nothing but what He reveals it to His servants the prophets first (Amos 3:7). This promise means you and I *can* know where the world is headed and not be shaken by what we see happening around us.

God has already given us "the rest of the story." You will find it in the awesome book of Revelation, a book that promises a special blessing to those who read it, hear what it says and order their lives accordingly.[1]

What a conversation starter it will become…

When those around you are walking
into God's judgment…

—⚅—

He's There—
Be Courageous,
Proclaim His Word

*I solemnly charge you in the presence of God and of Christ Jesus, who is to
judge the living and the dead, and by His appearing and His kingdom:
preach the word; be ready in season and out of season;
reprove, rebuke, exhort, with great patience and instruction.*

2 Timothy 4:1-2

Although Habakkuk questioned God, he didn't walk away. He waited to hear what God had to say. He was not disappointed, because God spoke. And Habakkuk learned some wonderful lessons, received a commission, and wrote it all down for us in a book!

If you, too, will learn to wait upon God, to get alone with Him, and to remain silent so that you can hear His voice when He is ready to speak to you, what a difference it will make in your

—⚅—

life! I think many of our problems overwhelm us simply because we do not set aside the time to be alone with God. I don't see how any Christian can survive, let alone live life as more than a conqueror, apart from regular quiet time alone with God.

So many voices are clamoring for our attention. So many philosophies and ideologies are thrown at us through our educational systems and numerous books. The radio, the television, or the CD player blares incessantly into many homes throughout the day and night. The Internet enables us to chat with people of all perspectives long into the darkness of night.

If we do not turn it all off and get alone with Him, how can we hear the still, small voice of God? "And after the earthquake a fire; but the LORD was not in the fire: and after the fire a still small voice" (1 Kings 19:12, KJV).

God is no respecter of persons. "God is not one to show partiality" (Acts 10:34). He will meet with us as He met with Habakkuk, if we will get alone and wait to hear what He says. "Wait for the LORD; be strong and let your heart take courage; yes, wait for the LORD" (Psalm 27:14).

Apparently Habakkuk did not have to wait long before God replied to his questions. Listen to what God said:

> Record the vision
> And inscribe it on tablets,
> That the one who reads it may run.

For the vision is yet for the appointed time;
It hastens toward the goal and it will not fail.
Though it tarries, wait for it;
For it will certainly come, it will not delay.
(Habakkuk 2:2-3)

Habakkuk was instructed to record the vision on a tablet so that others could read it. Theologians believe it was probably engraved on large clay tablets, which would be displayed in a public place such as the temple—or maybe even in the marketplace or city square. There it could be read by all. In this case, the reading of it placed a responsibility upon the readers: They were to run and proclaim it. Eventually, even you and I would read it!

When the Lord answered Habakkuk, He showed him what was to come in the future. The vision was yet for an appointed time. God assured Habakkuk that, although he would have to wait for it, it would not fail. It would come. According to God's timetable, the events presented in the vision would not be late. Whatever God says will come to pass *will* come to pass. Like it or not, want it or not, it is certain because God is certain. It may be a long time before it happens. It may be centuries, even a millennium or two. But if God says something will occur, then it will, because as He has "planned so it will stand" (Isaiah 14:24). At this point you may wonder why I am stressing this. Let me explain.

God was giving Habakkuk a glimpse of the future just as He

has given us a glimpse through His Word of what is yet to come. The Word of God clearly states over and over that Jesus Christ is coming to the earth "a second time...to those who eagerly await Him" (Hebrews 9:28). And when He comes to earth the second time, He will thoroughly deal with all of the ungodly.

Listen to what God spoke through the apostle Paul:

> For after all it is only just for God to repay with affliction those who afflict you, and to give relief to you who are afflicted and to us as well when the Lord Jesus will be revealed from heaven with His mighty angels in flaming fire, dealing out retribution to those who do not know God and to those who do not obey the gospel of our Lord Jesus. (2 Thessalonians 1:6-8)

It's always a delight to spread good news. Some people even take pleasure in spreading bad news about others. Few, however, delight to speak the news of God's judgment, especially if it not only pertains to others but to their own people! Why? Because no one wants to hear bad news. As a matter of fact, when people hear bad news, they often discredit both the message and the messenger.

No matter how people respond to the message, you and I are to proclaim it and live in the light of what we know of His coming and His judgment of the wicked, just as Habakkuk did. We are responsible to read and know the Word of God, which is so accessible, and then we are responsible to run to proclaim it. We need to proclaim and explain what we are learning in Habakkuk.

We need to share that, although God seemingly allows the wicked to prosper and destruction and violence to parade like conquerors through the cities of our land while justice is not upheld, there will come a day of reckoning. We need to clearly communicate that if people do not turn from their iniquity, they will experience the fierce wrath of Almighty God.

PROCLAIM THE TRUTH

To hear God's Word is to become accountable to it.

That is an awesome fact, one that you may not want to believe. But it is true. It does not matter whether you believe what God says or not, or even if you *like* what He says. You and I are accountable simply because God has spoken. It is as true for you and me as it was true for Habakkuk.

Consider this: When you stand before your God, will you have bloody hands, my friend?

When Paul told the elders at Ephesus, "I am innocent of the blood of all men. For I did not shrink from declaring to you the whole purpose of God" (Acts 20:26-27), what did he mean?

Paul was echoing a theme found in Ezekiel chapters 3 and 33. As we discussed earlier, there were three sieges of Jerusalem before it was finally destroyed in 586 B.C. You'll remember that

Ezekiel was taken by the Babylonians in the second siege of Jerusalem. His prophecy was written from captivity.

The following passage from Ezekiel will help you understand the gravity of knowing and proclaiming God's Word, whether people want to hear it or not.

> Son of man, I have appointed you a watchman to the house of Israel; whenever you hear a word from My mouth, warn them from Me. When I say to the wicked, "You will surely die," and you do not warn him or speak out to warn the wicked from his wicked way that he may live, that wicked man shall die in his iniquity, but his blood I will require at your hand. Yet if you have warned the wicked and he does not turn from his wickedness or from his wicked way, he shall die in his iniquity; but you have delivered yourself. Again, when a righteous man turns away from his righteousness and commits iniquity, and I place an obstacle before him, he will die; since you have not warned him, he shall die in his sin, and his righteous deeds which he has done shall not be remembered; but his blood I will require at your hand. (Ezekiel 3:17-20)

"Let the redeemed of the LORD say so" (Psalm 107:2). Proclaim it! Proclaim it, lest their blood be on your hands.

—⁓—

A LOVING CONFRONTATION

"I was ticked off by your message and I want you to know it."

That's an encouraging remark for a speaker to hear! My feelings were somewhat assuaged, however, when I heard this woman's reason.

She didn't agree with my stand on immorality.

She believed sex was fine outside of marriage even if you were married—as long as your partner consented! As a matter of fact, if she wanted to have sex with others, according to her there was nothing in the Word of God against it—as long as there was mutual consent. She told me I simply didn't understand the true meaning of adultery and fornication.

Besides all that, she didn't like my reference to having a religion without a relationship to God. And all of that "born-again talk" nauseated her!

The conversation went on for a while. Although she came on like gangbusters, I was excited. God had set a lost sheep right in my path in a one-on-one encounter. The thief was out to steal, kill, and destroy, but I knew the Shepherd wanted to say, "Here, sheepy, sheepy."

God's love welled up in my heart. I understood her rationalization of sin; I had once sat where she sat. But now I was silently praying, listening, and waiting.

Then I felt the timing was of the Spirit. I leaned over to her and said, "You are going to want to slug me, and I understand, but I have to be honest with you. My friend, you and I don't have the same Father. You're in darkness. You're deceived. You have a religion and not a relationship. Your father is the devil. You're going to hell."

I didn't have to duck, although I was prepared to!

The next day we had another conversation that lasted five hours. We talked until seven in the morning! This woman had come to blast one last word at me. Or so she thought. Our sovereign God had something else in mind.

As she continued to argue her beliefs on morality and the Word, I simply took her to one scripture after another, asking her to read each aloud. What was inscribed in God's Word, I proclaimed. Nothing else. Every time she wanted to argue, I simply said, "What does God say? Read it. Don't argue with me. He wrote it." All the while I groaned inwardly in prayer, asking God to open blind eyes and turn this dear soul from darkness to light.

Finally I said, "Why don't you get on your knees and tell God what you think about what you have read. Argue with *Him.*" We got on our knees. Her words turned to sobs, heaving out her sin. Suddenly she looked at me and said, "I feel so wicked, so desperately, desperately wicked. So despicable."

With tears in my eyes, I gently replied, "You are. You are desperately wicked. And what you have done is absolutely despicable. Tell God."

Well, what she formerly hated happened—she was born

again. Gloriously, wonderfully born again. Saved from the deepest of pits, from the cesspool of iniquity. As I sat there watching God be God, standing in awe of the new creation He had just brought into existence, over and over again I could hear in my heart Steve Green singing, "I have seen God's glory, I have lived and walked with Christ my Lord." And I had.

I tell you all this, beloved, because of what this woman said to me: "I need to talk to someone strong who will meet me on my level. Someone I can sort out the garbage with. Someone who will handle me like you did—who'll not back down, who'll understand, not run away in disgust, and yet say it in such love."

Years ago as I watched my friend Elizabeth McDonald, I learned how to speak the truth in love, how to lovingly confront people with God's impending judgment. Then as I matured in the Word, I saw what I had learned confirmed in the lives of Isaiah, Jeremiah, Ezekiel, and the other prophets. True prophets of God, those who serve as His spokesmen, do not dilute or alter His message. They're not dismayed by the response of their listeners. They warn of the just judgment of God, but they do it in love, in tears.

I grieve when I hear what I believe to be erroneous teaching that says, in essence, "Prophets are just straightforward and hard. That's their personality." A believer's personality is to be controlled by Christ. No matter our gifts or our calling, we are to be filled with His Spirit, manifesting His love, grace, and mercy along with His holiness, righteousness, and just judgment.

MAKING IT PERSONAL

Each of us is responsible to share our faith with others, for the Word says, "How then will they call on Him in whom they have not believed? How will they believe in Him whom they have not heard? And how will they hear without a preacher?" (Romans 10:14).

The circumstances of life, especially when bad things happen, give us divine opportunities to offer hope to those around us. One way to open a conversation is to give someone this book and then offer to discuss it with him or her.

I beg you, dear friend, to keep loving the lost; don't shut the door just because they aren't as "holy" as you are. After all, they don't have the same Father. Introduce them to yours by walking and loving just like your Father. Remember, Jesus ate with publicans and sinners; they were the ones who needed the Physician— and so do the hurting people in your life!

Now get out there and proclaim the good news. You have something greater than the cure for cancer; you have the antidote for death.

—◊—

He's There—You Can
Live by Faith

*But My righteous one shall live by faith;
and if he shrinks back, My soul has no pleasure in him.*

HEBREWS 10:38

We are so accustomed to living in an instant world that it is difficult to wait for anything.

When a significant event takes place somewhere in the world, a flick of the channel selector or a click of the mouse on a Web site will soon give us an instant rundown on the situation.

If we want something to gratify our appetite, there are plenty of fast-food places, or there is the frozen-food section in the grocery store and a microwave to heat or cook it in a hurry. Or we can just add water, then shake or stir.

If we want to buy something but don't have the cash, there are all sorts of ways to buy it on credit, and sometimes the payments

—◊—

won't even begin for several months. Yet we can have our product immediately.

As a society we have so promoted and provided instant gratification to the flesh that to deny ourselves *anything* seems almost cruel. We are no longer an immoral society; we're amoral. Anything goes as long as it makes man happy. There is no fear of God before our eyes.

Man is the center of his own world. What exists, exists for his pleasure. When he wants something, he goes after it. He'll get it for himself. He'll do it for himself. Self will be satisfied!

The prophet Habakkuk knew better than to get ahead of the Lord Almighty. After he had spilled out the questions of his heart, he did a very wise thing. He stood on his guard post, stationing himself on the rampart, and waited to see what God would say to him (Habakkuk 2:1).

Then, in the silence, in the expectant waiting, God spoke:

> Then the LORD answered me and said,
> "Record the vision
> And inscribe it on tablets,
> That the one who reads it may run.
> For the vision is yet for the appointed time;
> It hastens toward the goal and it will not fail.
> Though it tarries, wait for it;
> For it will certainly come, it will not delay.

> "Behold, as for the proud one,
> His soul is not right within him;
> But the righteous will live by his faith."
> (Habakkuk 2:2-4)

To Habakkuk, God gave the key to all of life, the key to the whole Word of God: The righteous, the just, will live by faith.

I want to show you why I, along with others, believe that Habakkuk 2:4 is the key verse of the entire Bible. Let's begin by looking at faith.

What does the Word of God mean when it speaks of faith? Faith is simply taking God at His Word. It is believing God. It is believing all that He says, whether you understand it or not, whether you can explain it or not. It is taking God at His Word, no matter how you feel, no matter how you read the circumstances, no matter what anyone else tells you about the truthfulness of what God says.

God *is* truthful. He does not lie. He cannot lie. Therefore, all that He says is truth. If anyone contradicts what God says, he is wrong. God's Word is truth. For that reason the very plumb line of our faith is the Bible, the unadulterated Word of God.

When the Word of God talks about faith, it means more than intellectual assent. The English transliteration of the Greek word for *faith* is *pistis,* meaning "a firm persuasion, a conviction based on hearing."[1] The word for *believe* is *pisteuō,* meaning "to be persuaded of, to place confidence in."[2] Biblical belief, then, signifies not mere credence of, but reliance upon, all that God says.

As you study God's Word, you see basically three elements involved in true faith or belief. They are (1) a firm conviction that fully acknowledges what God has revealed, (2) a surrender to what God has revealed, and (3) conduct that results from a personal surrender to what God has revealed.

The author of the book of Hebrews defines faith in this way: "Now faith is the assurance of things hoped for, the conviction of things not seen" (Hebrews 11:1). Under divine inspiration the author of Hebrews also gives us insight into a critical truth on which all of man's life and future pivot: "Without faith it is impossible to please Him, for he who comes to God must believe that He is and that He is a rewarder of those who seek Him" (Hebrews 11:6).

Therefore, if the just shall live by faith, the just must believe what God says, surrender to it, and live accordingly. Otherwise, they cannot please God.

FOOD FOR THE FAITHFUL

Now let's see where faith comes from. Romans 10:17 says, "So faith comes from hearing, and hearing by the word of Christ."

Faith is a firm persuasion, a conviction based on hearing.

Therefore, according to Romans 10:17, faith comes from hearing God's Word.

The Bible is God's Word to man. It is God-breathed and God-preserved from the time that Moses, under the moving of God's Spirit, began to write the Pentateuch to the time the apostle John completed the Scriptures by writing in the book of Revelation the things which were, which are, and which are yet to come.

When Jesus came to earth as the Son of Man, He never contradicted the Scriptures, nor did He ever imply they were inaccurate in any detail. What modern scholars have deemed mere stories recorded by man in order to illustrate a point, Jesus considered historical occurrences—events that actually took place.

The Bible is the Word of God. Can you now understand why God wrote what He did through Moses?

> He humbled you and let you be hungry, and fed you
> with manna which you did not know, nor did your
> fathers know, that He might make you understand that
> man does not live by bread alone, but man lives by every-
> thing that proceeds out of the mouth of the LORD.
> (Deuteronomy 8:3)

Consider Deuteronomy 8:3 in light of Habakkuk 2:4. It's obvious that if a man is to live by faith, he must believe everything that comes out of God's mouth and live accordingly.

Oh, my friend, never let anyone tell you God's Word contains errors. Won't you believe the sovereign, omnipotent, omniscient God? Won't you believe His Son, who is one with the Father and is called "The Truth"? Or will you believe men tutored by men over and above the testimony of the One who, as the Son of God, has been forever with the Father—the One who is called the very Word of God?

I believe the reason so many are failing today is that they have not disciplined themselves to read God's Word consistently, day in and day out, and to apply it to every situation in life.

Therefore, if you, dear child of God, are going to live by faith, you must feed on God's Word.

LIVING IN RIGHTEOUSNESS

Understanding Habakkuk 2:4 is literally a matter of life and death: eternal life or eternal damnation.

Habakkuk 2:4 is quoted three times in the New Testament: Romans 1:17; Galatians 3:11; and Hebrews 10:38. It is from these verses that we understand the magnificent sweep of the righteousness that we can have. Righteous means to be in right standing with God. Righteous living is life lived according to what God says is right.

Habakkuk 2:4 was used by New Testament authors in two ways. First, it was used in Romans 1:17 and Galatians 3:11 in relationship to salvation from the penalty of sin to show that salvation comes by faith and not by works. Second, it was used in Hebrews 10:38 in relationship to the believer's day-by-day salvation from sin's power as he walks by faith, believing and obeying God above all else.

This second aspect of the just living by faith is also seen in Romans 1:17: "For in it [the gospel] the righteousness of God is revealed from faith to faith; as it is written, 'But the righteous man shall live by faith.' " Salvation from sin—whether from the penalty of sin, which is eternal punishment, or from the power of sin's reign in our lives—is always and only by faith. There is no other way a man, woman, or child can be pleasing to God.

Galatians 3:11 says the same thing: "Now that no one is justified by the Law before God is evident." The Law can only expose sin. It can never make us righteous!

Righteousness comes only from God. It can never be attained by the flesh or by our self-righteous efforts. "He saved us, not on the basis of deeds which we have done in righteousness, but according to His mercy, by the washing of regeneration and renewing by the Holy Spirit" (Titus 3:5).

Think about it, dear Christian. What makes you acceptable to God? On what basis do you try to make yourself acceptable to God?

As you walk by faith, you live a righteous life because righteousness is always by faith.

As we've seen, the apostle Paul quoted Habakkuk 2:4 in his letter to the Roman believers. God used that statement to bring Martin Luther, a religious but lost monk, to salvation. His realization of the meaning of Romans 1:17 was then used to set multitudes free from the horrible bondage of a salvation-by-works religion into the glorious freedom of a salvation-by-faith relationship with God Himself.

As a monk, Martin Luther wished to obtain an indulgence promised by the pope to all who should ascend Pilate's Staircase on their knees. He was told that the steps had been miraculously transported from Jerusalem to Rome.

Luther kissed each step, begging God's mercy and forgiveness for the sins of his flesh, which tormented him. Suddenly, in the midst of performing this meritorious act, he thought he heard a voice of thunder cry from the bottom of his heart, *"The just shall live by faith."* As these words resounded unceasingly and powerfully within him, Luther rose in amazement from the steps up which he had been dragging his body.

The truth had set him free! Later he wrote:

Although I was a holy and blameless monk, my conscience was nevertheless full of trouble and anguish. I could not endure those words—"the righteousness of God." I had no love for that holy and just God who punishes sinners. I was filled with secret anger against Him: I hated Him because, not content with frightening by the Law and the miseries of life...He still further increased our tortures by the gospel.... But when...I learned how the justification of the sinner proceeds from the free mercy of our Lord through faith...then I felt born again like a new man; I entered...into the very paradise of God. Henceforward, also, I saw the beloved and Holy Scripture with other eyes.... As previously I had detested...these words, "the righteousness of God," I began from that hour to value and to love them.[3]

What do you think of the righteousness of God? Does it seem an impossible goal, never to be reached? Do you shudder at your own inability to be holy? Do you understand the righteousness that can be yours *only* if you believe in the Lord Jesus Christ?

Righteous means to be in right standing with God because your sins have been taken care of! When Christ hung on the cross, it was for your sins. There God "made Him who knew no sin to be sin on our behalf, so that we might become the righteousness of God in Him" (2 Corinthians 5:21).

At the moment of faith, the moment of trusting in Christ's substitutionary death for your sins, you are declared righteous; you are put in right standing with God. Imagine! You, like Martin Luther and every other true child of God, begin to live anew. The just shall live by faith!

But that is just the beginning! You are saved by faith from sin's ultimate penalty, which is eternal death in the lake of fire. Once that birth takes place, you are to walk by faith.

This second aspect of the righteous living by faith is emphasized in Habakkuk 2:4 and in Hebrews 10:38. Both Habakkuk and the recipients of the book of Hebrews were living in difficult times, times of testing. In those times, as always, there was only one way to live, and that was by faith. To think you could live any other way, under any other religious system, philosophy, reasoning, or thinking, would be prideful. "Behold, as for the proud one, his soul is not right within him; but the righteous will live by his faith" (Habakkuk 2:4).

No matter what the trial, no matter what the circumstances, you and I are to live by every word that proceeds out of the mouth of God—without compromise. We are to trust and obey because there is no other way.

LAY DOWN YOUR PRIDE

Did you ever expect something from God and find yourself disappointed, even grieved, by His response? Maybe a situation wasn't resolved in the way you thought it should be or when you thought it should be.

Many Christians say that all we have to do is claim things in faith, believe they are ours, make a positive confession, and they will come to pass. And if things don't come out the way you have claimed them or confessed them, it's because you don't have enough faith or because someone else has hindered the work of God through a negative confession.

I don't believe such thinking is biblically based. It does not concur with the whole counsel of the Word of God.

Habakkuk could have made a positive confession every minute on the minute, but it still wouldn't have changed his circumstances. He could have praised God in faith, claimed victory over the forces of Satan, and demanded in prayer that the Babylonians be prevented from coming against Judah, but it would not have altered what was about to take place. Yet some Christians today would say that Habakkuk dropped the ball. They would say things could have been different if Habakkuk had only had enough faith, claimed the right promises, prayed the right prayer, and said the right things.

God will not be manipulated. He does not conform to us or to our estimation of life. Rather, we are to bow the knee in faith and know the sovereign "LORD is in His holy temple. Let all the earth be silent before Him" (Habakkuk 2:20).

When my father had to go into the hospital for surgery on an aortic aneurysm, I asked God for a scripture concerning him. I felt God gave me Psalm 20 and, with it, the assurance that my sixty-eight-year-old father would not die. But almost a month later, after five major operations within twelve days, Daddy died.

WHEN BAD THINGS HAPPEN

I wasn't there. I left him in the intensive care unit with my mother at his side and returned to my family in Chattanooga, believing that he would live.

I felt that I had the Word of God regarding my father. But I was wrong. Daddy died. Had my faith failed? Had God failed? What went wrong?

Nothing went wrong. I simply misunderstood God.

Do you feel that something should be happening in your life that isn't? Or has something happened that you think God shouldn't have allowed? Are there cries or pleas that God doesn't seem to respond to? In the light of what you are learning in Habakkuk, are you going to allow this to throw you into a chasm of distress or despair?

Read Isaiah 40:27 aloud, and put your name in place of Israel's and Jacob's. Then listen to God's response in 40:28-31 by reading it aloud also.

> Why do you say, O Jacob, and assert, O Israel,
> "My way is hidden from the LORD,
> And the justice due me escapes the notice of my God"?
> (Isaiah 40:27)

> Do you not know? Have you not heard?
> The Everlasting God, the LORD, the Creator of
>   the ends of the earth

Does not become weary or tired.
His understanding is inscrutable.
He gives strength to the weary,
And to him who lacks might He increases power.
Though youths grow weary and tired,
And vigorous young men stumble badly,
Yet those who wait for the LORD
Will gain new strength;
They will mount up with wings like eagles,
They will run and not get tired,
They will walk and not become weary.
(Isaiah 40:28-31)

Faith recognizes that God is in control, not man.

Faith does it God's way, in God's timing—according to His good pleasure.

Faith does not take life into its own hands, but in respect and trust it places it in God's.

This is the contrast between "the proud one [whose] soul is not right within him" and the righteous one who "lives by faith." Faith waits and trusts, taking God at His Word. Pride moves according to its own desires, its own will. Pride does what it wants to do, when it wants to do it, and the way it wants to do it!

How are you living, my friend—in faith or in pride? "The righteous will live by his faith" (Habakkuk 2:4).

What will you do when life is difficult to understand? When doubt pounds on the door of your mind, calling you a fool for not letting him in? When believing God seems insane? When human reasoning lays before you the rational choices of the majority of thinking men and women?

Will you follow the logical choices of man, or will you seek your God in prayer, waiting to see what He will say? And when His answer comes, will you cling to His Word in faith?

When things become difficult, even unbearable, will you change your mood with the tide of circumstances, or will you rejoice in the God of your salvation? In the trial of your faith, will you turn to the arm of flesh, or will you allow God to be your strength? Will you stumble in the darkness of your own reasoning and in the logic of the blind leading the blind, or will you let God help you walk above the difficulties of life?

Listen to Jeremiah 17:5-8:

> Thus says the LORD,
> "Cursed is the man who trusts in mankind
> And makes flesh his strength,
> And whose heart turns away from the LORD.
> For he will be like a bush in the desert
> And will not see when prosperity comes,
> But will live in stony wastes in the wilderness,

A land of salt without inhabitant.
Blessed is the man who trusts in the LORD
And whose trust is the LORD.
For he will be like a tree planted by the water,
That extends its roots by a stream
And will not fear when the heat comes;
But its leaves will be green,
And it will not be anxious in a year of drought
Nor cease to yield fruit."

Every difficulty is a test—a test to see whether you will believe God, a trial to drive you into His arms and His promises, where you find Him all-sufficient. That is what the book of Habakkuk is about.

In Habakkuk we see the difficulty of wondering where God is when bad things happen. Then we witness the delight of discovering that He is there, ruling over all.

Like Habakkuk, all we have to do is lay down our pride… and choose to live by faith.

MAKING IT PERSONAL

How are you handling life? Are you trying to do it all yourself, striving to figure it out, make it work as you push and shove, maneuver and manipulate? Do you really think you can make it work by yourself? Oh, beloved, you can't do a thing—you can't even breathe—without God's permission.

Quit striving and remember He is God. Rest in the knowledge that His grace is sufficient, His power is perfected in weakness.

Why don't you just sit down, lean back, take a deep breath and say, "Father, nothing matters but that I please You. And I know that without faith it is impossible to please you. Those who come to you must believe that You are God. Without You I can do nothing. With You all things are possible. This is the faith You reward. May I pursue the goal in faith and hear your 'Well done' from the grandstand of heaven."

When you are angry about the injustice
in the world, remember…

—⟶⟶—

He's There—Woe
to the Wicked

*The proud look of man will be abased, and the loftiness of man will
be humbled, and the LORD alone will be exalted in that day.*

ISAIAH 2:11

No cruelty, no crime, no injustice escapes the attention of God. He is there when bad things happen. And although God may use evil men or ungodly nations to judge His people or to carry out His eternal purposes, they will be held accountable for what they have done.

The wicked will be punished. This is clearly stated in Habakkuk: "I am raising up the Chaldeans, that fierce and impetuous people who march throughout the earth to seize dwelling places which are not theirs…. Then they will sweep through like the wind and pass on. But they will be held guilty, they whose strength is their god" (Habakkuk 1:6,11).

This fact was a part of the vision Habakkuk was to record

—⟶⟶—

and others were to proclaim. The Lord would justly deal woes to those who treated men like fish, worshiped the nets that caught the fish, and swallowed up those more righteous than they (Habakkuk 1:13-17). Judgment will come when God goes forth for the salvation of His anointed.

We'll see this in the third chapter of Habakkuk. However, for the moment we need to look at the taunt-song against the Babylonians, a song for those who are proud and behave as the Babylonians behaved (Habakkuk 2:6). The taunt-song has five stanzas of three verses each. This type of song is called a *masal,* which is Hebrew poetry employing parallelism. In the taunt-song you'll gain valuable insight into a side of God often neglected: His wrath and just judgment.

God sets before Habakkuk the way of life and death—and the consequences of man's choices. For those who walk by faith, there's life. For those who are proud, there are woes and death. We can learn much from these woes. Knowing what Habakkuk says regarding the fate of the wicked will help you understand where God is when bad things happen. You'll see that He's not divorced from your pain. Everything that concerns you is His business! He's not a distant Creator who brought you into being and then abandoned you, saying, "Good luck growing up, kid. Hope you do all right." He is not only your Creator, He's also your Sustainer.

So when you wonder where God is when bad things happen, remember:

1. God is in control. He rules over all. He's in charge of history…yours as well as the nations!

2. All history centers on two groups of people: Israel and the Church. If you are in Christ, because He is in you, then you are a vital part of the Church, a member of Jesus' body.

3. There is a purpose in what God is doing, whether we see it or not. You have God's promise on that. What happens may not be good, but because He is God, He'll cause it to work together for your good.

4. Your times are in His hands. He's in charge of the timetable, so wait patiently.

5. Fear and doubt are conquered by a faith that rejoices. And faith can rejoice because the promises of God are as certain as God Himself.

And where do the woes fit in? They come under the third principle: *There is a purpose in what God is doing. He is acting according to His character.*

Although Habakkuk could not understand why God allowed the Babylonians to be His instrument of judgment upon His people Israel, God had a purpose in it all. He would use the Babylonians to judge. Yet, in His righteousness, God would also judge the Babylonians.

Although you, my friend, cannot understand why God did not intervene on your behalf in the midst of your trauma, you must believe God had a purpose. And if evil was done to you, it will be judged. Evil must come, but woe to those by whom it comes.

So as you look at these woes, remember that although they are pronounced against the Babylonians, they pertain to all who behave likewise. God is immutable; He never changes. He is consistent not only in blessing the righteous but also in judging sinners—whoever they are!

WOE TO THE GREEDY

Greed is subtle. It begins with the lust of the eyes as it contemplates what it would be like to possess more things, more power, more of anything. You can come to a point where you must take from others to satisfy your own appetite. Confronting this appetite in man, God pronounced the first of the woes on the wicked:

> Will not all of these take up a taunt-song against
>   him,
> Even mockery and insinuations against him
> And say, "Woe to him who increases what is not
>   his—
> For how long—
> And makes himself rich with loans?"
> Will not your creditors rise up suddenly,
> And those who collect from you awaken?

Indeed, you will become plunder for them.
Because you have looted many nations,
All the remainder of the peoples will loot you—
Because of human bloodshed and violence done
　　to the land,
To the town and all its inhabitants.
(Habakkuk 2:6-8)

In the *King James Version* the word *covetousness* is used to translate the original Hebrew word for *greed.* In essence greed and covetousness are one and the same. Covetousness is expressly forbidden in the Ten Commandments: "You shall not covet your neighbor's house; you shall not covet your neighbor's wife or his male servant or his female servant or his ox or his donkey or anything that belongs to your neighbor" (Exodus 20:17).

The Babylonians coveted what the other nations had, so they went after it—and brutally wrenched it from the homes of the people they conquered. They took things they had not labored or saved for. They stole other men's wives and children for their own pleasure and service. They hauled away treasures that belonged to families, treasures that held precious memories. They wasted homes, forests, property, but mostly they wasted lives. They left a trail of blood, all because of greed. They were totally occupied with self—their pleasures, their happiness, their comfort, their conveniences. What they had didn't satisfy them. It wasn't enough.

When the Babylonians took what was not theirs, they became the debtors. The people they stole from were the creditors. The Babylonians owed a debt to those they looted. Eventually the debt would be paid, because God is a just judge.

You may believe you have little in common with the Babylonians, but let me ask you, my friend, how do you view money and the accumulation of earthly possessions? Have you ever stopped to think about it? Since we are looking at the woes of those who seek to make themselves rich at the expense of others, I think we need to consider the Christian's attitude toward wealth and treasures.

Is it a sin to be rich, to possess material things? Let's discover what the Word of God has to say.

Look at 1 Timothy 6:7-12,17-19:

> For we have brought nothing into the world, so we cannot take anything out of it either. If we have food and covering, with these we shall be content. But those who want to get rich fall into temptation and a snare and many foolish and harmful desires which plunge men into ruin and destruction. For the love of money is a root of all sorts of evil, and some by longing for it have wandered away from the faith and pierced themselves with many griefs.
>
> But flee from these things, you man of God, and pur-

sue righteousness, godliness, faith, love, perseverance and gentleness. Fight the good fight of faith; take hold of the eternal life to which you were called, and you made the good confession in the presence of many witnesses.

Instruct those who are rich in this present world not to be conceited or to fix their hope on the uncertainty of riches, but on God, who richly supplies us with all things to enjoy. Instruct them to do good, to be rich in good works, to be generous and ready to share, storing up for themselves the treasure of a good foundation for the future, so that they may take hold of that which is life indeed.

When Paul tells Timothy to "flee from these things," he is referring to more than the love of money. But since greed is our subject, let's keep our focus there.

Have you ever thought of greed as a form of idolatry?

That's what God calls greed in the New Testament. Listen: "Therefore consider the members of your earthly body as dead to immorality, impurity, passion, evil desire, and greed, which amounts to [literally, is] idolatry. For it is because of these things that the wrath of God will come..., and in them you also once walked, when you were living in them" (Colossians 3:5-7).

Interesting, isn't it? When we think of idolatry, we usually think of people worshiping images fashioned by their own hands.

—᙮᙮—

Or we think of sticks, stones, or fetishes of one sort or another. But greed? If it were not stated in the Word of God, would anyone think of it as idolatry? Probably not, unless we recognize an idol as anything that takes God's rightful place in our allegiance, devotion, time, or energies.

WOE TO THOSE WHO TAKE ADVANTAGE OF OTHERS

Has the company you've worked for all these years suddenly fired you when you were on the brink of retiring? Have they pocketed your retirement funds so they can save their own neck financially?

Has your home ever been robbed? Has anything ever been stolen from you? Have you ever been swindled? Woe upon that person, for he did exactly what the Babylonians did to Judah.

Has anyone ever told a lie about you to keep you from something or someone he wanted?

Has anyone ever put you down so he could look better?

Do you think these things escape the notice of a holy God who neither slumbers nor sleeps but beholds all the affairs of men from His throne on high?

The second woe is against those who seek their own security at another's expense:

> Woe to him who gets evil gain for his house
> To put his nest on high,

To be delivered from the hand of calamity!
You have devised a shameful thing for your house
By cutting off many peoples;
So you are sinning against yourself.
Surely the stone will cry out from the wall,
And the rafter will answer it from the framework.
(Habakkuk 2:9-11)

The Babylonians thought that by destroying others and strengthening their own kingdom, they would secure themselves against the aggression of other nations. They forgot it is God who "removes kings and establishes kings" (Daniel 2:21).

This second woe condemns self-exaltation, the putting of one's self above another for the sake of your own good, your own benefit, your own security.

How contrary to the example we have in our Lord Jesus Christ! The mind of Christ is the opposite of pride or self-exaltation. It is laying aside selfishness and regarding others as more important than ourselves. It is taking on the role of servant rather than that of master. It is laying down your life for another.

While woe comes upon those who exalt themselves at the expense of others, God promises blessing for those who don't. Read Philippians 2:3-11, which follows this paragraph. Read it prayerfully. Ask God to show you if you need cleansing through this portion of His Word.

Do nothing from selfishness or empty conceit, but with humility of mind regard one another as more important than yourselves; do not merely look out for your own personal interests, but also for the interests of others. Have this attitude in yourselves which was also in Christ Jesus, who, although He existed in the form of God, did not regard equality with God a thing to be grasped, but emptied Himself, taking the form of a bond-servant, and being made in the likeness of men. Being found in appearance as a man, He humbled Himself by becoming obedient to the point of death, even death on a cross. For this reason also, God highly exalted Him, and bestowed on Him the name which is above every name, so that at the name of Jesus EVERY KNEE WILL BOW, of those who are in heaven and on earth and under the earth, and that every tongue will confess that Jesus Christ is Lord, to the glory of God the Father.

Are there any aspects of your attitude or your relationships with others in which you've been more like the Babylonians than like Jesus? Allow the Lord to search your heart. He'll do it in love. He simply wants a clean temple.

As we conclude our study of the second woe, we need to remember: When greedy men build their own houses through evil gain and at the expense of others, people will cry out, "Where is

God?" Our answer to them is that the very stones of the house will cry out and the rafters will answer. Habakkuk 2:11 tells us that whatever was obtained through evil will testify against the evildoer. There is *nothing* hidden which will not be brought to light.

WOE TO THE VIOLENT

Listen and note how this third woe follows upon the other two: "Woe to him who builds a city with bloodshed and founds a town with violence! Is it not indeed from the LORD of hosts that peoples toil for fire, and nations grow weary for nothing?" (Habakkuk 2:12-13).

How does this apply to us today?

Those who watch network television for more than two hours on any given night rarely escape being exposed to violence and bloodshed. The statistics concerning the amount of violence and crime seen by the average child before he reaches puberty are constantly increasing from one year to the next—and have become alarming. Is it any wonder our children are desensitized to violence and evil at a very early age? And when the television is turned off and they go to their toy boxes or play their video games, does the exposure to violence cease? Sadly, no.

You cannot take in all that violence, profanity, and immorality without it searing your conscience to some degree and influencing your perspective on life. What the eyes and ears take in, the mind and heart feed upon. Here again we see that as a man thinks, so he is (Proverbs 23:7).

Consider Matthew 15:18-19 in the light of the subjects we've been discussing. Why are we plagued with teenage immorality, pregnancies, and abortions? Why are condoms recommended to teens and not abstinence? It is because we have become an amoral society. Man and his pleasures have moved God from His rightful place. We have slain the absolutes of God upon the altar of our lusts. We have abandoned purity.

As a nation where well over one million babies are aborted every year, isn't ours a land filled with bloodshed? Isn't it violent to destroy what God has chosen to weave in a mother's womb, what's been given life by God's own breath (Psalm 139:13-16)?

Where is God? Why does He allow these crimes against humanity to continue? Why does our justice system put people who protest such bloodshed and violence in jail, yet turn murderers and rapists loose to murder and rape again? Why do the wicked seem to be victorious in all the wanton bloodshed left on the trail of their own pursuit of happiness?

Habakkuk asked God the same questions:

How long, O LORD, will I call for help, and You will not hear? I cry out to You, "Violence!" Yet You do not save. Why do You make me see iniquity, and cause me to look on wickedness? Yes, destruction and violence are before me; strife exists and contention arises. Therefore the law is ignored and justice is never upheld. For the wicked surround the righteous; therefore justice comes out perverted. (Habakkuk 1:2-4)

Then came the vision…and Habakkuk understood.

And someday everyone will understand, for the earth will be filled with the knowledge of the glory of the Lord, as the waters cover the sea. Someday men will see that the Lord was in His holy temple all the time. God knew what was going on.

Men and nations may build their domains through violence and bloodshed, but there will be a day of reckoning. God says that they are toiling for fire (Habakkuk 2:13).

What they gain will someday be destroyed. God will devour it in judgment. For "the day of the Lord will come like a thief… and the elements will be destroyed with intense heat, and the earth and its works will be burned up" (2 Peter 3:10).

And when the earth is destroyed, those who don't know Christ—whether they be kings or ordinary people, slaves or free—will be cast into the lake of fire where the worm will not die, and the fire will not be quenched. There they will remain for all eternity (Matthew 25:41,46; Mark 9:44,46,48; Revelation 20:11-15).

There's one final thought I must share with you. Violence and bloodshed are not always the end product of greed. You'll find that frequently violence and bloodshed come from anger.

Anger is never to control us. Although God is fully aware of the injustice and cruelty of men, He says, "Be angry, and yet do not sin; do not let the sun go down on your anger, and do not give the devil an opportunity" (Ephesians 4:26-27). If you allow anger to stay within, if you don't act in faith and deal with it in God's way, it can destroy you and others. As I said, it can even lead to violence and bloodshed. For that reason Jesus tells us, "Everyone who is angry with his brother shall be guilty" (Matthew 5:22). Anger that simmers within is like committing murder in your heart.

Oh, beloved, others may have committed evil or unrighteous acts against you. Your anger may be righteous anger. But if your soul is going to be right within you, if you are going to live by faith, then you must forgive. Give your anger to God, and believe Him when He says it will work together for your good in order to make you more like Jesus (Romans 8:28-29).

Just remember: Anger unresolved will only bring you woe.

WOE TO THOSE WHO LEAD OTHERS INTO SIN

The fourth woe is taken up as a taunt-song against those who entice others and seduce them for their own benefit. It's a woe not only to the Babylonians, but also to every human being who uses another for his own pleasure—to every drug dealer; to every producer, publisher, and seller of pornography; to every person who encourages another to have a drink; to every person who goads another until he joins him in his evil deeds.

It is a woe to every person who has beaten, verbally abused, or sexually misused another person...and who in the process destroys lives, leaving them devastated and barren apart from God's grace. It is a woe not only to the drunken Babylonians who excused their behavior in the name of conquest, but to every person who might think that, because he was drunk, he was not responsible for his behavior.

Listen once again, dear friend, to the vision God gave Habakkuk. Read it and hurry to proclaim it before society is totally destroyed:

> Woe to you who make your neighbors drink,
> Who mix in your venom even to make them
> > drunk
> So as to look on their nakedness!
> You will be filled with disgrace rather than honor.
> Now you yourself drink and expose your own
> > nakedness.
> The cup in the LORD's right hand will come
> > around to you,
> And utter disgrace will come upon your glory.
> For the violence done to Lebanon will over-
> > whelm you,

And the devastation of its beasts by which you
    terrified them,
Because of human bloodshed and violence done
    to the land,
To the town and all its inhabitants.
(Habakkuk 2:15-17)

While I believe Habakkuk's fourth woe goes beyond simply describing drunkenness and refers to the exposure of Babylon and her judgment as a nation, it is interesting that God uses her love and abuse of wine to illustrate what He's going to do. This isn't the first time Habakkuk has mentioned alcohol in reference to the Babylonians. In 2:5 we read that "wine betrays the haughty man, so that he does not stay at home."

Usually people who drink do not want to drink alone, unless, of course, they are afraid they'll be found out. Drinking and drunkenness were acceptable to the Babylonians. From Habakkuk 2:15 we see that they even enticed their neighbors to join in. What was their motive? To look on another's nakedness.

Where you find alcohol abuse, you often find immorality and destruction. When a person drinks excessively, he usually loses his inhibitions. The alcohol controls the person rather than the person controlling the alcohol.

The violence and destruction that many times go hand in hand with alcohol are seen in Habakkuk 2:17, where God says,

"For the violence done to Lebanon will overwhelm you, and the devastation of its beasts by which you terrified them, because of human bloodshed and violence done to the land, to the town and all its inhabitants." When the Babylonians conquered Lebanon, they wantonly destroyed Lebanon's people and animals. They also destroyed Lebanon's beautiful forests, leaving just tree stumps.

Have you ever been around people who were drunk? Sometimes they are sadly humorous. Other times they're embarrassingly obnoxious—or cruel and abusive.

Proverbs 23:29-35 gives a graphic description of the effects of too much drink.

> Who has woe? Who has sorrow?
> Who has contentions? Who has complaining?
> Who has wounds without cause?
> Who has redness of eyes?
> Those who linger long over wine,
> Those who go to taste mixed wine.
> Do not look on the wine when it is red,
> When it sparkles in the cup,
> When it goes down smoothly;
> At the last it bites like a serpent
> And stings like a viper.
> Your eyes will see strange things
> And your mind will utter perverse things.

And you will be like one who lies down in the
    middle of the sea,
Or like one who lies down on the top of a mast.
"They struck me, but I did not become ill;
They beat me, but I did not know it.
When shall I awake?
I will seek another drink."

So what should be the Christian's relationship to wine or strong drink?

We know from Ephesians 5:18 that we are not to be "drunk with wine, for that is dissipation." Dissipation means to be out of control. The Christian is never to be out of the control of the Holy Spirit. You cannot be filled with the Holy Spirit and be under the influence of alcohol. Joy and peace do not come from alcohol; they come from obedience to the indwelling Spirit of God.

Though Scripture clearly condemns drunkenness as sin, as far as I know, nowhere does the Bible expressly forbid drinking wine. But does the absence of such a command allow you or me the liberty of drinking wine?

Let me share with you what I believe. My belief is based on Romans 14:21-23:

It is good not to eat meat or to drink wine, or to do anything by which your brother stumbles. The faith which

—∞—

you have, have as your own conviction before God.
Happy is he who does not condemn himself in what he
approves. But…whatever is not from faith is sin.

A Christian cannot drink wine unless he can do it with a clear
conscience before God while at all times adhering to the clear
teachings of God's Word. If a Christian does feel the liberty to
drink wine, then he must be controlled by the law of love. His
drinking should never cause another to stumble.

WOE TO IDOLATERS

The final woe in Habakkuk's taunt-song is against idolaters. As
you read it, remember idolatry occurs when a person removes
God from His rightful place of preeminence and puts something
or someone else in that place. Habakkuk writes:

> What profit is the idol when its maker has carved it,
> Or an image, a teacher of falsehood?
> For its maker trusts in his own handiwork
> When he fashions speechless idols.
> Woe to him who says to a piece of wood,
>   "Awake!"
> To a mute stone, "Arise!"
> And that is your teacher?

Behold, it is overlaid with gold and silver,
And there is no breath at all inside it.
(Habakkuk 2:18-19)

Idols may be symbolized or personified in a carved image of wood, a molded image of gold, silver, or some other material, or in a stick, stone, or some object of nature. The idols of America are not as easy to spot as the icons of Old Testament times or the fetishes of superstitious people who still worship other gods. Idols do not always take on some definitive form—especially in our day, age, and culture. But never doubt that they are just as real. They are just as damning.

It does seem ridiculous to worship something you have made with your own hands, doesn't it? And yet, aren't we equally as ridiculous when we listen to and worship the words and the works of other finite human beings while ignoring the living, inerrant Word of God?

I am always amazed at the audacity of men who sit in judgment on the truth of the Word of God. How can man be wise enough to tell us what parts of God's Word are from God and what parts are merely the invention of man's own will? I am floored by those who set themselves up as critics of the Old Testament, calling much of it myths or mere stories told to convey spiritual concepts.

Jesus said, "O foolish men and slow of heart to believe in all that the prophets have spoken!" (Luke 24:25). Did He not explain to the men on the road to Emmaus, "beginning with Moses and with all the prophets,...the things concerning Himself in all the Scriptures" (v. 27)?

Our Lord never sought to correct, change, or add to God's Word. Instead, He confirmed its veracity over and over again. Do you think putting the reasoning of man, the writings of man, the wisdom of man, the psychology of man, the philosophy of man, the understanding of man, the experience of man, or the teaching of man above the Word of God might be considered idolatry? Romans 1:21-23 says it is! They worshiped and served the creature—man—rather than the Creator.

Why is God against idolatry? Because its focus is on what man creates rather than on the Creator. Because of this idolatry, man is ensnared by Satan, who is a murderer, liar, and destroyer.

God loves us and desires our highest good. He made us for Himself. And His name is *Qanna,* which means "jealous." God is jealous for us. We tend to think of jealousy as something evil. Yet there is a good and proper jealousy. A husband or wife has every cause to be jealous if his or her mate is giving affection and attention to another. And it is the same with God.

Nothing—no person, no object—is to take His rightful place in our affections or our attention. Think about it. Does He have the preeminence in your affections? Do you desire Him above all else and everyone else? Could you live without anyone but Him? Or have others—idols—crowded Him out so that you live for others above Him, seeking to please them above your God? And what priority do you give Him? How much of your attention does He receive? Do you talk with Him daily? weekly? monthly? annually? Do you take vacations *from* God or *with* God?

Take a moment and think about these things. They are critical questions. Be objective. If you have idols in your life, you must realize they are as great a sin as adultery or murder. Hear, oh, hear the word of the Lord in Exodus 20:3: "You shall have no other gods before Me." Have you? "You shall not worship them or serve them; for I, the LORD your God, am a jealous God, visiting the iniquity of the fathers on the children, on the third and the fourth generations of those who hate Me, but showing lovingkindness to thousands, to those who love Me and keep My commandments" (Exodus 20:5-6).

If there are idols in your life, how are others who watch you going to see "the LORD is in His holy temple" (Habakkuk 2:20)? His temple is not only in heaven but also is in you. As part of the Church of Jesus Christ, you are His earthly temple. Clean God's temple; rid it of its idols. Let others see your uncompromising passion for Christ—and be silent before Him.

M A K I N G   I T   P E R S O N A L

Whenever we hear truth, beloved, we become accountable for what we know and how we live in light of it. Jesus tells us that God's Word becomes our judge (John 12:48). We also learn from 2 Corinthians 5:10 and Romans 14:10 that all Christians will stand before the judgment seat of Christ and give account for the deeds done in our flesh, whether they be good or bad.

In the light of this—and of God's command in Ephesians 5:15-16 for us as believers to be careful how we walk, continually making the most of our time because the days are evil—why don't you keep a general log for two weeks of where and how you spend your time each day? Then review it objectively to see if you've put anything before God. If you find this to be true, if anyone or anything is receiving the attention and affection that ought to be reserved for your heavenly Father, then it is an idol—and you know what to do with idols: Get rid of them.

When you cannot seem to go on...

He's There—You Can Walk with Hinds' Feet

Be strong and let your heart take courage, all you who hope in the LORD.

PSALM 31:24

If you're like me, your spirit is troubled at the blindness of men. It is my heart's desire to open the Word of God under His anointing and to share the truth in love so that people know what is coming if they don't repent. I long for people to be confronted in a way that causes them to think twice before they blatantly, needlessly rush headlong into iniquity and eventual destruction!

If you know God's Word and don't have your head buried in the sand of your own little world, then I am sure you can understand and relate to my frustration. What can we—you and I—do?

This is the question Habakkuk was asking. He knew what was going on, and it frustrated him. His recourse is ours: God.

We must lay our questions, frustrations, anxieties, and impotence at the feet of God and wait for His answer. When we receive it, we must live by faith.

God assured Habakkuk—and therefore assures us—that the ungodly would not go unpunished; woes were determined and would not fail. But somehow the knowledge of coming judgment is not enough. There is one more thing we need to be assured of, and this truth is God's final reassuring word to Habakkuk. The world may be worshiping idols, justice may be perverted, wickedness may abound, strife and violence may be the order of the day...but God is not like the idols, who cannot speak.

Habakkuk had God's assurance that He is in His holy temple. He has pronounced His woes. Sin will be judged. His judgment will come. It will not fail. Let all the earth hush. They have no rebuttal, no excuse, no justified complaint, nothing to say to God. The wisdom and cleverness of man have failed. Man's impotence is obvious, his judgment sure.

The truth that balances the knowledge of coming judgment is the fact that God is God—immutable, eternal—and that all is under His control! You can rest because what He has planned for Israel and for the Church will come to pass. Keep silent, O world.

And you, child of God, live by your faith. You can! Faith will hold because it is faith in the everlasting Sovereign Ruler of all the universe, the Creator of heaven and earth, the One who sits on the throne. He's in His holy temple!

I do not know your trials or your frustrations. I can't know what might be troubling you or making you anxious. But God knows those things. What you don't understand, what you feel unable to cope with, can be overcome moment by moment if you will live by faith and walk in communion with Him.

In Habakkuk 3, we see the "prayer of Habakkuk the prophet, according to Shigionoth" (3:1). We also come across the word *Selah* in verses 3, 9, and 13. Although no one seems to be certain about the precise meaning of these terms, let's take a few minutes to look at what I have gleaned from others regarding the meaning of *Shigionoth* and *Selah.*

The singular term for *Shigionoth*—*Shiggaion*—is used in the introduction of Psalm 7. According to the footnote in the *New American Standard Bible,* a Shigionoth is "dithyrambic rhythm or a wild, passionate song." Others say it refers to the kind of music that accompanied the song. Since the word comes from a verb meaning "to err," the thought is one of a song sung in great excitement, a triumphal song.[1]

Selah, which occurs seventy times in the psalms and three times in this chapter, indicates a heightening of the musical accompaniment, the musical forte. It allows for a pause and meditation.[2]

Why don't you pause now and read this passage.

After reading Habakkuk 3, can you see why this is a prayer according to Shigionoth? The Lord will come for the salvation of His people. Now that's something to get excited about!

Habakkuk finally saw beyond the immediate circumstances troubling him. He realized that although God was going to use the godless Babylonians, there was a purpose in what God was doing. He was fulfilling His sovereign plan—for Israel and for the nations.

Israel would be judged through the Babylonian invasion and captivity, but that was not to be the end of Israel. God would revive His work in the midst of the years. In wrath He remembers mercy, because like Himself, His ways are everlasting.

As before, God will come from Teman. He will go forth for the salvation of His anointed as He marches in indignation through the earth and tramples the nations (Habakkuk 3:2-3,6,13).

Although the present and the near future looked bleak, it was only temporary. God's promises for Israel would stand. Nothing could ever change them. They would not fail. Habakkuk's God was the everlasting One who does not change but keeps His covenants.

Once Habakkuk understood what God was going to do, he seemed to urge God to move ahead with His plans. He said to the Lord, "Revive Your work in the midst of the years, in the midst of the years make it known" (Habakkuk 3:2).

Once you understand that God judges wickedness, that He will bring it to a halt, and that He will exalt righteousness and vindicate the righteous, aren't you anxious to have God get on with His plans? I want wickedness to be stopped. I hate what man is doing to man. It burdens me that the innocent suffer because of the ungodly deeds of a perverse generation.

As I sat and talked with a young mother the other day, we discussed how crucial it is these days to watch our children virtually every minute we are out in public. Why? Because there are so many people stealing children right out from under parents' eyes.

I remember the story of a couple who went to Disney World with their two children. One was in a stroller, the other walking beside mommy and daddy. Suddenly their little girl was missing. They panicked.

As they went for help, the police at Disney World told them to split up and go stand at two different exits while they closed all the other exits. As they stood at the gates, they were told to look straight into the eyes of each child leaving the park.

Time passed, seeming to drag on into eternity. But they continued to obey the police and looked carefully into the eyes of each child. Finally a couple approached the gate with their weary child asleep on the father's shoulder. The child was covered with a blanket. The parents of the sleeping child didn't seem bothered when asked to pull back the blanket.

As the child was nudged and awakened, they looked into her drowsy, sleepy eyes. The parent of the lost little girl knew they had found their child. The clothes were not the same. Their daughter was dressed as a boy. Her pretty hair was gone. It had been cut like a boy's and even dyed another color, but the child was theirs.

I remember the freedom of my childhood, playing unattended outside, walking to the corner store. The young mother I talked with remembers being dropped off at the mall for a few hours. But today many parents don't allow their children to enter a public restroom unattended. When Jack and I take our grandchildren out, they never leave their Mimi or Pa's side.

How we long for God to revive His work! We want men to again fear God and tremble before Him. We want our Lord to hurry and come. Even though it means judgment to the wicked, it will bring salvation to the righteous.

Oh, my friend, are you in pain? hurting and confused? His coming will bring all of that to an end. God's own hand will wipe away all your tears. Justice will reign supreme. So pray for the peace of Jerusalem—for the Deliverer to come out of Zion.

He has said, "Yes, I am coming quickly." May your prayer and mine be, "Amen. Come, Lord Jesus" (Revelation 22:20).

KINDNESS AND SEVERITY

"In wrath remember mercy" (Habakkuk 3:2). This is Habakkuk's cry as he hears of God's coming judgment.

At God's bidding, the Babylonians would sweep down upon Judah. Habakkuk could not help but fear. Weakness entered his bones, and he trembled because he "must wait quietly for the day of distress, for the people to arise who will invade us" (Habakkuk 3:16). And yet, as we have just seen, he *wanted* this day of distress to come, for sometime after that day the Lord would come for the salvation of His people. The Babylonians—and eventually every other wicked nation—would be threshed or trampled by God (3:12-13). Therefore, Habakkuk prayed, "O LORD, revive Your work in the midst of the years, in the midst of the years make it known" (3:2).

In Habakkuk 3 we behold the kindness and severity of God (Romans 11:22)—severity in judging sin, kindness in redeeming His chosen people. Habakkuk, looking beyond the just but severe wrath of God, awaited His coming for the salvation of His own. Although some feel God is through with Israel because of their rejection of the gospel, God's Word teaches us that

> a partial hardening [against the gospel] has happened to Israel until the fullness of the Gentiles has come in; and so all Israel will be saved; just as it is written,
>
> "THE DELIVERER WILL COME FROM ZION
>   [a reference to the heavenly Zion],
> He will remove ungodliness from Jacob."
> "This is My covenant with them,
> When I take away their sins."
> (Romans 11:25-27)

The Deliverer who is to come from Zion is the same deliverer Habakkuk describes in 3:3-15. He is the same One referred to in Jeremiah as "the righteous Branch." He is the "Son of Man" referred to in Daniel 7:13-14:

> I kept looking in the night visions, and behold, with the clouds of heaven one like a Son of Man was coming, and He came up to the Ancient of Days and was presented before Him. And to Him was given dominion, glory and a kingdom, that all the peoples, nations and men of every language might serve Him. His dominion is an everlasting dominion which will not pass away; and His kingdom is one which will not be destroyed.

Habakkuk awaited the deliverance of God, remembering God's deliverance in the past when He brought the Israelites out of Egypt, took them through the wilderness, and brought them into the land of Canaan. He remembered when God caused the sun to stand still so that Joshua could win his battle.

The One who mightily delivered in the past, judging Israel's enemies in His wake, was the same One who would deliver them again and again, until all was in subjection under His feet.

Don't you stand in awe of God and His ways? Doesn't it give you great confidence to know that the gifts and the calling of God are irrevocable? God's dealings with Israel, His patience and persistence, His loving-kindnesses, His fulfillment of His Word—all testify to the fact that He will act in the same, consistent way with you. Think about it. It should bring you peace even as it did Habakkuk when he couldn't understand what God was doing.

A Quiet Waiting

When God does not seem to answer you or move on your behalf, when you cannot seem to go on, what do you do?

This, beloved, is the fourth major truth you need to keep before you: *Your times are in God's hands.* He's in charge of the timetable, so wait patiently. This fact sustained Habakkuk, and it will sustain you when there seems no relief in sight and when you are weak and weary of fighting the good fight, of running the race with endurance.

As we read those last magnificent and unparalleled words of faith in Habakkuk 3:16-19, we see that Habakkuk had contented himself with God's timetable. He states, "I must wait quietly for the day of distress, for the people to arise who will invade us" (3:16). The Lord was in His holy temple and Habakkuk could be silent. He could wait quietly. Habakkuk's resignation was not of defeat but of faith. He went on to say that he would rejoice in the God of his salvation.

God does not want compliant resignation. When life is difficult, God wants us to have a faith that trusts and waits. He wants us to have a faith that does not complain while waiting but that rejoices because we know our times are in His hands—nail-scarred hands that labor for our highest good.

—∾—

Corrie ten Boom was a single woman who ended up in Hitler's extermination camps because she and her family hid Jews in their home in Holland during World War II. Her release from that camp was a miracle only to be followed by another—her worldwide ministry.

At the age of ninety-one, five years before her death, our sovereign Father allowed Corrie to suffer a stroke that left her speechless. The woman who cared for Corrie in those years wrote, discussing

> why God had allowed this illness to take place. We wondered, talked, and prayed on the subject, but never came up with a complete answer to the mystery. We felt there was a lot we did not understand about why God allows suffering. What came to us in increasing measure was an assurance of the absolute sovereignty of God. Of vital importance to me was the growing realization that our times were completely in God's hands. He knew the length of Tante Corrie's life. It did not depend on anything except His will.

Corrie's daily prayer was: "Lord, keep me close to Your heart so that I see things as it were more and more from Your point of view."[3]

This, beloved, is my prayer for you and for me as we joyfully surrender in faith to the truth that our times are in His hands. In doing so, I know we will find Him to be our strength even as He was Corrie's.

A FAITH THAT REJOICES

That story leads us to the fifth and final truth to brand on your heart: *Fear and doubt are conquered by a faith that rejoices.*

Praise is the spark plug of faith. Praise gets faith airborne, where it can soar above the gravitational forces of this world's cares. The secret of faith is continual praise even when your inward parts tremble, your lips quiver, and decay enters your bones.

When Corrie ten Boom and her sister Betsy were taken to a German concentration camp, they were ordered to strip naked and pass before the watching eyes of German soldiers. Some women today would not be affected by this demand. But to these two godly women who had been sheltered in the purity of a home where Christ was honored without compromise, this was a horrifying experience. Not only were they enduring great humiliation, there was also the terror of the unknown. They knew they were considered enemies.

How did they endure? How did they keep from totally losing their inner peace as they stood naked before eyes filled with curiosity, anger, or blatant lust? Betsy turned to Corrie and told her that they were going to rejoice in the fellowship of His sufferings.

She reminded Corrie that Jesus, too, had been stripped naked and exposed to the eyes of men at Calvary.

And rejoice they did—time and time again. Oh, humanly there was nothing to rejoice about, but there was Someone in whom they could rejoice! Their fear and doubt were conquered by a faith that enabled them to rejoice—no matter what their circumstances or their future.

They did what Habakkuk did. Listen to his words: "Yet I will exult in the LORD, I will rejoice in the God of my salvation" (3:18).

Oh, dear one, when you doubt, when iniquity abounds, when you want to question God, there are two things you need to do. First, run immediately into the ever-open arms of your Father. You have welcome access to the embrace of your omnipotent, sovereign God. There is no need to look to the arm of flesh. In faith, fling yourself into all that He is, into all that He has said.

Second, rejoice in Him. In a sense, rejoicing activates your faith because you are saying, "Father, You are all that I need. You are the One in whom I trust 'though the fig tree should not blossom and there be no fruit on the vines, though the yield of the olive should fail and the fields produce no food, though the flock should be cut off from the fold and there be no cattle in the stalls'" (Habakkuk 3:17).

When you fling yourself in faith into all that God is and into all His Word says, when you rejoice in Him in the face of every circumstance, then you will know His strength. His strength will enable you to walk with hinds' feet on high places. Hinds' feet do not slip. Isn't that wonderful! Most often it is in the difficult times that Christians stumble. They turn to the arm of flesh, to something or someone other than God, and in the process they turn from Him. And the arm of flesh is not the answer. A person who does not cling to God's Word in faith will find his life dry and barren (Jeremiah 17:5-6). But…

> Blessed is the man who trusts in the LORD
> And whose trust is the LORD.
> For he will be like a tree planted by the water,
> That extends its roots by a stream
> And will not fear when the heat comes;
> But its leaves will be green,
> And it will not be anxious in a year of drought
> Nor cease to yield fruit.
> (verses 7-8)

What is God saying to us in Jeremiah? He wants us to see the same thing that Habakkuk saw. Though difficulties, trials, and testings come, though temporal blessings fail, we can overcome if we will cling to God in faith. He is our strength. You and I can have green leaves in drought and bear fruit if our roots run deep in faith.

Precious friend, when you find yourself in difficult and trying situations, do not be proud and try to handle life in your own strength. Live by faith. Exult in the Lord. Rejoice in the God of your salvation. He is able to deliver you from—and through—any difficulty of life.

I know, beloved, that it is not easy to rejoice when you find yourself in the midst of devastating circumstances. It seems like insanity. But you are not to rejoice in the circumstances, but in the God who is in charge of the circumstances!

With the apostle Paul, you can say, "Not that I speak from want, for I have learned to be content in whatever circumstances I am. I know how to get along with humble means, and I also know how to live in prosperity; in any and every circumstance I have learned the secret of being filled and going hungry, both of having abundance and suffering need. I can do all things through Him who strengthens me" (Philippians 4:11-13). God is fully adequate!

In your trial, this is what you need to remember:

God is in control. He is in charge of history because He is sovereign.

History centers on the Jewish people and the children of God.

There is a purpose in what God is doing, whether or not you see or understand it.

Your times are in His hands.

And your fear and doubt will be conquered by a faith that rejoices.

We can rejoice in our circumstances because we are looking not at them but at Him. Oh, beloved, your faith will become airborne when you "consider it all joy...when you encounter various trials" and when in faith you are "always giving thanks for all things" (James 1:2; Ephesians 5:20). Truly, this is how "the righteous will live by his faith" and, in doing so, he will discover that "the Lord GOD is my strength, and He has made my feet like hinds' feet, and makes me walk on my high places" (Habakkuk 2:4; 3:19).

Habakkuk's days were draped in darkness, just as yours may be. But the darkness did not overwhelm him! In faith he pulled back the curtains and saw the rising Son, coming in glory to dispel the dark night of the soul.

Where is God when bad things happen? He's behind the curtains, directing, and overseeing it all. Walk with hinds' feet on faith's mountaintops!

MAKING IT PERSONAL

If God is just behind the curtains, then you can know He is waiting to hear your declaration of faith, your belief that He is sovereign over all. So when He puts you on stage, don't forget your lines; the people watching need to see a faith that walks with hinds' feet on God's high places.

The high places He ordains for us are often places of affliction, times of tribulation, for in this life, at this period in eternity, we are put to death all day long, we are accounted as sheep for the slaughter:

> But in all these things we overwhelmingly conquer
> through Him who loved us. For I am convinced that nei-
> ther death, nor life, nor angels, nor principalities, nor
> things present, nor things to come, nor powers, nor
> height, nor depth, nor any other created thing, will be
> able to separate us from the love of God, which is in
> Christ Jesus our Lord. (Romans 8:37-39)

Let me encourage you to do two things that will help this truth remain foremost in your thoughts and life—even when bad things happen. First, memorize Habakkuk 3:17-19. Second, determine that whatever comes your way, the first thing you will do is give thanks to God that He is sovereign. Rejoice that this trial, tragedy, crisis—whatever it is—has been filtered through His fingers of love and will be used to make you more like His Son, our blessed Savior, Jesus Christ.

"For I consider that the sufferings of this present time are not worthy to be compared with the glory that is to be revealed to us" (Romans 8:18).

Notes

—∞—

HE'S THERE, LISTENING TO THE CRY OF YOUR HEART

1. On page 551 of the *New Inductive Study Bible*, see the chart, "Israel's Division and Captivity." You can call your Christian bookstore to order the *New Inductive Study Bible* (a Gold Medallion–winner among study Bibles), which is published by Harvest House. Or you may write Precept Ministries International, P.O. Box 182218, Chattanooga, Tennessee 37422, or call 800-763-8280.

HE'S THERE—TELL HIM YOU'VE PLAYED THE FOOL AND RUN TO HIS ARMS

1. From time to time we will look at the definition of a word in the Greek or Hebrew. Since the Old Testament was originally written in Hebrew and the New Testament was originally written in Koine Greek, sometimes it is helpful to go back to the original language to see the meaning of a word. There are many study tools to help you if you would like to do this type of digging. One excellent book to help you understand how to

do more in-depth study is *How to Study Your Bible* (Eugene, Ore.: Harvest House, 1994).

HE'S THERE—THERE'S A PURPOSE IN IT ALL

1. If you're interested in studying this further, you may want to purchase a copy of the International Inductive Study Series on Revelation: *Behold, Jesus Is Coming* (Eugene, Ore.: Harvest House, 1995).

HE'S THERE—YOU CAN LIVE BY FAITH

1. W. E. Vine, *Expository Dictionary of Old and New Testament Words,* 2 vols. (Old Tappan, N.J.: Revell, 1981), 2:71.
2. Vine, *Expository Dictionary*, 1:116.
3. J. H. Merle D'Aubigne, *The Life and Times of Martin Luther* (Chicago: Moody, 1978), 54-6.

HE'S THERE—YOU CAN WALK WITH HINDS' FEET

1. Charles L. Feinberg, *The Minor Prophets* (Chicago: Moody, 1951), 216.
2. Feinberg, *The Minor Prophets,* 217.
3. Pamela Rosewell, *The Five Silent Years of Corrie ten Boom* (Grand Rapids: Zondervan, 1986), 85.

About Kay Arthur and Precept Ministries International

—⁓—

Kay Arthur, executive vice president and cofounder of Precept Ministries International, is known around the world as a Bible teacher, author, conference speaker, and host of national radio and television programs.

Kay and her husband, Jack, founded Precept Ministries in 1970 in Chattanooga, Tennessee. Started as a fledgling ministry for teens, Precept today is a worldwide outreach that establishes children, teens, and adults in God's Word, so that they can discover the Bible's truths for themselves. Precept inductive Bible studies are taught in all fifty states. The studies have been translated into sixty-five languages, reaching 118 countries.

Kay is the author of more than 120 books and inductive Bible study courses, with a total of over five million books in print. Four of her books have received the ECPA Gold Medallion Book Award. She is sought after by groups throughout the world as an inspiring Bible teacher and conference speaker. Kay is also well known globally through her daily and weekly television programs.

Contact Precept Ministries for more information about inductive Bible studies in your area.

Precept Ministries International

P.O. Box 182218

Chattanooga, TN 37422-7218

800-763-8280

www.precept.org

Printed in the United States
by Baker & Taylor Publisher Services